the POWER of
SPIRITUAL
THINKING

GORDON FERGUSON

the POWER of SPIRITUAL THINKING

DPI

DISCIPLESHIP
PUBLICATIONS
INTERNATIONAL

The Power of Spiritual Thinking
© 2000 by Discipleship Publications International
One Merrill Street, Woburn, Mass. 01801

Printed in the United States of America

———————————————————————

ISBN: 1-57782-138-6

Cover Design: Jennifer Matienzo
Interior Design: Christine Nolan

Dedication
To Aleea Hope Klinkhammer

I remember clearly my father's comment about grandchildren as he played in the floor with his: "You haven't really lived until you have grandchildren." Dad was right on that one, no doubt about it. Two years ago, your aunt and uncle, Bryan and Joy, had little Bryce, and then your parents, Jeff and Renee, had you, giving us both a grandson and granddaughter—our cup runs over as grandparents!

The writer of Proverbs said it well: "Children's children are a crown to the aged." The psalmist's prayer has come true in our lives, "May you live to see your children's children," and now our prayer in response is found in Psalm 103:17: "But from everlasting to everlasting the Lord's love is with those who fear him, and his righteousness with their children's children."

Welcome, little Aleea Hope, into a family that prays daily for you and your cousin to become disciples of our Lord Jesus. You are our special little angel from God.

Contents

Introduction
The Power of Positive Thinking

Many years ago I read a very popular book of the day entitled *The Power of Positive Thinking* by Norman Vincent Peale, a well-known religious leader. The idea of the book was that success and happiness in life are only available to those who learn to think positively. He used many appropriate Biblical passages to make his points. Anyone in the world, including the nonreligious, who accepted his premises would be blessed by doing so because positive thinking is certainly superior to negative thinking. However, we must ask the question of how positive thinking relates to spiritual thinking. Although the two share much in common, they are definitely not equivalent to one another.

Much of the positive thinking touted in the world is based on selfish means to selfish ends. We are taught to think positively in order to be successful in a worldly way—to get what we want. Only in a secondary manner are others blessed by such an approach. Biblically, positive spiritual thinking has as its main goal pleasing God and serving others. Therefore, happiness is not something we seek via positive thinking; it is the by-product of being spiritual. But what is spirituality? Generally, people are confused about what true spirituality is, and they often mistake another quality for it. The following illustration should help clear up this confusion.

Imagine yourself at a reception of a business associate where the hostess, knowing that you are a "religious type," introduces you to a denominational minister. Picture this man of the cloth as being like the stereotypical minister in old movies, complete with soothing voice, subdued personality and very gentle demeanor. As you try to converse with him, he talks about his work in almost ethereal tones. Later, as you are leaving the reception, the hostess whispers in your ear, "Isn't he just so spiritual?"

Now imagine yourself at a gathering of religious types in a church building, where something like a church fundraising sale is taking place. People are dickering over the asking prices, voices are raised, some of the buyers seem agitated, and money is clutched tightly in the sweaty palms of almost everyone present. In walks a man who observes the unruly gathering with a look of amazement on his face, then seems to be seething inside as his look turns to anger. He deliberately walks over to the tables being used by the cashiers, grabs them one by one and dumps their contents at the feet of the startled cashiers. Loudly, he renounces their religious hypocrisy, claiming that this place of worship and study is not to be viewed and treated as a common flea market. Would anyone observing him whisper in your ear, "Isn't he just so spiritual?"

Thus we see the challenge of determining what true spirituality is. What the world generally deems to be spirituality is actually a sentimental brand of piety, the quality we saw in the first example. The second example was, of course, an updated version of Jesus as described in John 2. In popular thinking, a pious person is someone who speaks soothing and innocuous thoughts of God and fulfills religious obligations. Biblically, spirituality is simply doing the will of God with the right motivation behind the obedience. Read the following words from 1 Corinthians 2:

> This is what we speak, not in words taught us by human wisdom but in words taught by the Spirit, expressing spiritual truths in spiritual words. The man without the Spirit does not accept the things that come from the Spirit of God, for they are foolishness to him, and he cannot understand them, because they are spiritually discerned. The spiritual man makes judgments about all things, but he himself is not subject to any man's judgment. (1 Corinthians 2:13-15)

Since the Holy Spirit has inspired the words, embracing them in both heart and action is the same as being led by the Spirit. To be filled with the Spirit means that we are filled with his words, not simply in our minds, but in our hearts and behavior. Spirituality, then, is accepting the stated principles of God until they become an ingrained part of our characters—not just in what we do, but what we are. Spirituality is becoming like the spiritual God of the universe.

Before we accepted the ways of God, we followed the paths of the world—stated more bluntly, the ways of Satan. We would expect the two paths to be diametrically opposed, and they are. However, Satan is the master deceiver and he camouflages his path to make it look both attractive and correct. After years of being deceived in our concepts of right and wrong, we should not be surprised that developing spiritual thinking is challenging at best and often downright difficult. The blessings of learning to imitate God are in direct proportion to the difficulty involved. As Paul and Barnabas went about "strengthening the disciples and encouraging them to remain true to the faith," they uttered this classic statement: "We must go through many hardships to enter the kingdom of God" (Acts 14:22). The more we learn to be positive spiritual thinkers, the more we will become like Jesus and the more spiritually successful we will be. But the process is not easy.

The goal of this book is to help you unlock some of the doors of true spirituality. As was the case with my last book, *The Power of Gratitude*, this volume is not intended to be an exhaustive examination of a subject, but merely a collection of brief chapters to stimulate you toward a better understanding and practice of it. The feedback from the little book on gratitude has been most gratifying because it has served its purpose to prompt more thankfulness to

God, the giver of all blessings. May he help this book on spiritual thinking to achieve the similar goal of encouraging more people to think spiritually and to thereby gain the divine power that he offers. To that end it is written and to that end my prayers accompany it, as it is introduced to you, the reader. Enjoy—and God bless!

1 A Forgiving Spirit

"So watch yourselves.

"If your brother sins, rebuke him, and if he repents, forgive him. If he sins against you seven times in a day, and seven times comes back to you and says, 'I repent,' forgive him."

The apostles said to the Lord, "Increase our faith!"

Luke 17:3-5

Cultivating a forgiving spirit is one of our greatest challenges. Some people are better at forgiving than others, for whatever reason, but all of us have more difficulty forgiving in some circumstances than in others. For example, just about any parent will find it easier to forgive something done against them rather than something done against their children. We are very quick to defend our children—partly to rightly protect them and partly to wrongly protect our own pride. Further, we find it more difficult to forgive someone who hurts us repeatedly. No wonder Jesus' call for unlimited forgiveness (seven times in a day) was met with the apostles' plea to increase their faith!

Obviously, being able to quickly forgive is our goal, for that is the example of God. I have seen people work through the process of forgiveness and reconciliation in different ways. Some do forgive quickly. Once they hear and see evidence of godly sorrow, they are settled out and full of sympathy for the repentant sinner. At the other end of the spectrum are those who are very tedious in their attempts to forgive. They seem to want to untangle every possible strand of what went wrong, and the process is often laborious and slow. The latter type typically experience ongoing relationship difficulties because they are far too concerned with determining who sinned the most rather than focusing on reconciliation.

In the Luke 15 account of the runaway son, God, represented by the father in the story, shows us what a forgiving spirit is all about. The son had rehearsed the speech he planned to deliver to his father.

> "I will set out and go back to my father and say to him: Father, I have sinned against heaven and against you. I am no longer worthy to be called your son; make me like one of your hired men."
> (Luke 15:18-19)

But when he actually spoke to his father, before he could get out the last sentence, he was interrupted.

> "But the father said to his servants, 'Quick! Bring the best robe and put it on him. Put a ring on his finger and sandals on his feet.'" (Luke 15:22)

Once God sees that we have godly sorrow and are set on repenting, he is ready to forgive and begin the celebration of reconciliation. How much are we like him when we have been hurt? Without a willingness to forgive, we cannot be forgiven by God. (See Matthew 6:14-15 and 18:23-35 for some chilling admonitions to this effect.)

Many years ago, I heard a preacher in my old denomination say that his God was bigger than we are and could forgive us, whether we forgave others or not. When I repeated the statement to another preacher, he replied succinctly: "Well, then, his God must be a liar!" The message of Scripture is too clear to miss. Not only must we forgive those who sin against us, but we must also forgive in the way that God forgives (Colossians 3:13). He forgives quickly, completely, repeatedly—and then forgets the sins (Hebrews 8:12). This means that he never allows our past mistakes to influence negatively his current view and treatment of us, and he never brings them back up. Now, imitate that type of forgiveness, and with the apostles, cry out, "Increase our faith!"

I have recently discovered an alarming tendency some have regarding forgiveness. They evidence a reasonably forgiving spirit toward those outside the kingdom of God who hurt them, but they easily become bitter toward those in the kingdom who hurt them. In one sense, this is understandable. We expect more of disciples, and since we open ourselves up more to them emotionally, the sins against us go far deeper into our hearts and hurt much more. Psalm 55:12-14 gives us insight into the nature of this pain in these words:

> If an enemy were insulting me,
>   I could endure it;
> if a foe were raising himself against me,
>   I could hide from him.
> But it is you, a man like myself,
>   my companion, my close friend,
> with whom I once enjoyed sweet fellowship
>   as we walked with the throng at the house
>   of God. (Psalm 55:12-14)

The difficulty of forgiveness in such cases is described in Proverbs 18:19.

> An offended brother is more unyielding than a
>   fortified city,
> and disputes are like the barred gates of a
>   citadel.

No matter how great the challenge of forgiving trusted brothers and sisters may be, it is part and parcel of the Christian life. The church is perfect on the divine side, having been planned by God, but it is imperfect on the human side. Human beings sin, even saved ones, and disciples are going to hurt other disciples and sin against them. This is certain, as much as all of us wish it were different. Therefore, we must not only strive to avoid sinning against each other, but we must also learn to forgive as God forgives.

My favorite passage dealing with forgiveness is one that ties in going the way of the cross with surrendering our personal hurts: 1 Peter 2:18-24. Since it is such a foundational passage, let's take the time to read it carefully before proceeding further.

> Slaves, submit yourselves to your masters with all respect, not only to those who are good and considerate, but also to those who are harsh. For it is commendable if a man bears up under the pain of unjust suffering because he is conscious of God. But how is it to your credit if you receive a beating for doing wrong and endure it? But if you suffer for doing good and you endure it, this is commendable before God. To this you were called, because Christ suffered for you, leaving you an example, that you should follow in his steps.

> "He committed no sin,
>   and no deceit was found in his mouth."

> When they hurled their insults at him, he did not retaliate; when he suffered, he made no threats. Instead, he entrusted himself to him who judges justly. He himself bore our sins in his body on the tree, so that we might die to sins and live for righteousness; by his wounds you have been healed.
> (1 Peter 2:18-24)

Many essential lessons about enduring hurtful treatment are found in these verses. First, our response to others must have nothing to do with how they treat us. This should not be surprising, when we remember that the word almost always used for "love" in the New Testament is *agape*, and by definition *agape* love is unconditional. Even if someone is harsh toward us, we are to respond with *all* respect, not because of who they are but because of whose we are. It may be extremely difficult to show respect to a harsh person, but it is a decision we are called to make—"submit yourselves" (verse 18). In verse 20, enduring harsh treatment is much more than gutting it out; it is accepting such treatment with both grace and respect toward the offender.

Second, our response to those who mistreat us must be based on the example of Jesus, for we are called to follow in his steps. He was sinless and deserved no ill treatment. Yet, he responded to it without retaliation by entrusting himself to God. He knew that God was in control and would bring good out of an evil situation and accomplish his purposes. It is a matter of surrendering to the ultimate control of an Almighty God.

Third, our response when we are hurt is the catalyst that can induce repentance in those who have hurt us. Jesus had many followers during his personal ministry because of the miracles he performed, but they were scattered when he was arrested and sentenced. However, when he died in the way he did, without retaliation and with a prayer on his lips for those killing him, everything changed. People were drawn to him like a magnet. It was the message of the cross that had the power to convert the thousands, even in periods of intense persecution. How we accept ill treatment is the whole issue here. The more we suffer with grace and mercy toward our offenders, the more they are drawn to God. It is the way of the cross!

Now, let's go on to 1 Peter 3 for further applications of the principle. In verses 1-6, women are instructed to go the way of the cross with their husbands ("in the same way"). The husbands appear to be non-Christians in this context, although the principles apply to Christian spouses as well. In spite of how wives might be treated, they are to respond with a gentle and quiet spirit. They are to be submissive to their mates, no matter what their mates seem to deserve. In verse 6, we find a very important part in this submission: The wives are not to give way to fear. What does this mean? It means that they will not reason as non-Christians reason in such cases, thinking that submission will mean that they will be mistreated and taken advantage of. They may well be treated badly in the short term, but surrender to the control of God allows God to change the offender, the husband, in the long term. The way of the cross works, although it may not work quickly. For example, how long did it take Jesus' cross to break down your walls of sin?

Next, in 1 Peter 3:7, husbands are also instructed to follow the principle of the cross—"in the same way." In this context, the wives appear to be Christians, but again, the principles apply either way. Husbands are to be considerate of their wives, treating them with respect, regardless of how the wives may be responding to the husband's leadership. Love is unconditional, which means that the way of the cross must be followed whether or not the wives are living righteously and respectfully with their husbands.

In many sessions of marriage counseling, we find couples who feel justified in their unrighteousness because of the sins of their mates: "Well, he did thus and so, which is why I did what I did." *So what?* What do our mates' actions have to do with our responses? Absolutely nothing—if we are intent on being disciples and following the example of Jesus! Of course, this is far easier said than done, but it must be done. Taking up our crosses means that we suffer at the hands of others, even our mates, without retaliation and with respect. If we do this, the offenders will be melted by our gentleness, and they will hopefully repent. Even if they do not, our righteous responses will give them the best opportunity to repent.

Now look at 1 Peter 3:8-9. With the word "finally," it is obvious that Peter is continuing the theme of the previous verses—his application of the way of the cross. First in the chapter, wives with non-Christian husbands are addressed; next, husbands with Christian wives; and then, all disciples with each other. In verse 8, we are told to treat one other with sympathy, love, humility and compassion, which results in harmony. In verse 9, we are told to go the way of the cross by responding to insults with blessing. We could assume that here Peter switches to a consideration of how we respond to non-Christians, but I think it is not a necessary assumption. Even if he does, the principle would surely apply to our response to fellow Christians. Love is unconditional toward our enemies—how much more important that unconditional love be shown toward our brothers and sisters in Christ!

Taking the way of the cross accomplishes two very important things in God's plan. First, it refines our characters, making us more like Jesus. Even in the popular passage about God working all things together for good (Romans 8:28), God goes on to tell us that the good he has in mind is to conform us into the image of Jesus (Romans 8:29). Suffering is God's greatest tool to produce Christlikeness in our characters (Romans 5:1-5, James 1:2-4, Hebrews 12:5-11). In that sense, the greater the pain inflicted on us, the greater the potential to grow. Rather than becoming bitter because we were hurt by other disciples, seize the opportunity to respond righteously and to grow tremendously as a result.

Second, taking the way of the cross also works on those who sin against us by bringing them to repentance. Forgiving a small hurt softens the one forgiven in probably a small way. Forgiving them for a large hurt has the potential to soften them in a larger way. Therefore, the greater the hurt forgiven, the greater the impact on the one forgiven. Both the forgiver and the forgiven benefit in direct proportion to the depth of the sin which is responded to righteously. The *Via Dolorosa* is indeed the "way of suffering," as the song says, and it is the most powerful tool in the world to change human beings. It is Christ's way and it must be our way, for it is ultimately the path to forgiveness for all of us.

To Help You Focus

1. Where does your forgiveness fall on the spectrum, ranging from easy to difficult? What does your best friend say?

2. Which scripture in this chapter was the most convicting for you and why?

3. Think back to a time when you needed to forgive someone of something you considered big. How did you feel before you said, "I forgive you"? How did you feel afterward, seeing their reaction?

4. Why do you have great confidence in "the way of the cross"?

The Rest of the Story

He who answers before listening—
that is his folly and his shame.
Proverbs 18:13

The heart of the discerning acquires
knowledge;
the ears of the wise seek it out.
Proverbs 18:15

The first to present his case seems right,
till another comes forward and
questions him.
Proverbs 18:17

Paul Harvey, well-known commentator, hosts a radio program called "The Rest of the Story." He begins by presenting a scenario of an unusual human-interest story and when the suspense is built up sufficiently, he delivers the punch line, which is always unexpected, often amazing and sometimes shocking. Similarly, whenever dealing with conflict, the other side of most stories we hear can be just as unexpected and shocking—hence the huge importance of hearing both sides of anyone's story in order to have a true, spiritual perspective.

I recall the first marriage counseling I did as a young minister. The wife came to my office first and described her marriage problems to me. As I took notes, I found myself thinking that her husband was a real lout who needed a swift kick in the pants! The next day I met with the husband, and as he began describing his marriage, I thought to myself, "Some mistake has been made; he must be someone else's husband." Since I had not known them before, I honestly thought that I was dealing with two different marriages. I tried to inconspicuously see the names written on my notes to find out if they were married to each other or not—and sure enough, they *were*! This lesson was not lost on me: Do not reach firm conclusions without hearing both sides of any story!

Proverbs 18:17 has more applications than we usually imagine. The most obvious may be in the marriage counseling setting. And on this point, let me say that this principle applies even in situations when one mate is a disciple and the other is not. We are all too prone to hear the disciples' sides and assume that they are accurate in their assessment simply because they are Christians. Remember the cardinal rule of discipleship: Assume nothing!

Another application of the principle involves how we form opinions of others based simply on our observation of their actions in one given situation without delving into the background behind those actions. For example, on numerous occasions, I have had conversations with people who have been disturbed by something they have seen in me (or thought they had seen). To my amazement, they had formed a very strong opinion about my heart and motivations without ever even talking to me and hearing my side of it. Yet, their approach with me was highly conclusory in nature—operating as a one-man judge and jury, such people so trust their opinions that they come to me with very definite conclusions. Not only is such an approach exceedingly arrogant, it is Biblically unloving because it constitutes a flagrant violation of the Golden Rule. How much better it would be to come in a humble, loving manner, searching for the truth, with an approach which would strengthen the relationship rather than straining it. Humility in such situations would prompt a disciple to say something like this: "I have seen something which concerns me, but I haven't heard your side of it yet. Please help me understand what is going on." Then you will find out the rest of the story, and it may well considerably change your conclusion.

Yet another application of Proverbs 18:17 involves how we reach decisions, especially as leaders, be it in the home, the world or the church. A good leader has the humility to realize that he does not know everything about every subject. Hopefully, he even has the humility to realize that he does not know nearly as much as he thinks he does. In other words, he knows that he can be wrong and that he assuredly does not know how to choose between good, better and best consistently without the help of others. A one-man-show type of leader violates

Proverbs 18:17 from the very outset in what he thinks leadership is all about. He decides everything himself, and it all seems very right, especially to him in his self-contained system of reasoning. The wise leader, on the other hand, initiates the *process* of making decisions, gathering input from those who can best help. He may well make the final decision himself, but not until he is satisfied that he has gathered all of the pertinent facts upon which to base the decision. Not only will those being led appreciate being valued as team members, but the decisions will also be consistently very good.

Perhaps one of the most needed applications of our principle of hearing the rest of the story is more subtle and very often overlooked. We can have far too much confidence in our own side of the story and be reticent or even resistant to trusting another's perspective which differs from ours. It's good to be perceptive about people and situations. The ability to be perceptive comes from both experience and from natural gifts. However, the more perceptive we are, the more prone we are to be prideful and to trust our judgment too much.

Many years ago, I made a trip to Florida to visit the Crossroads church, since it was the leader in the campus ministry movement among mainline Churches of Christ at the time. This church was not only fast-growing, it was controversial—very controversial in the minds of most leaders in those churches. But, in my attempt to practice the Proverbs 18:17 principle, I went to see things firsthand. The trip went well and I learned a lot. I came to the conclusion that most (not all) of the controversy was not connected to reality. Church leaders whose own work paled in comparison to that being done by the Crossroads church were jealous and threatened by anything that violated their traditions.

I returned from that trip eager to share what I had seen and learned with other leaders in my home city. I knew that many of these church leaders attended a monthly preacher's luncheon and normally heard from a guest speaker. Although I did not often attend these meetings, I called the man responsible for planning the program and asked if I could speak at the next luncheon. He informed me that another speaker had been asked already, but that he would try to postpone his speech until a later luncheon. As it worked out, I was able to speak about my visit to the church in Florida. Knowing the strength of the controversy in my home area churches, I was careful to report what I had seen in a factual, nonemotional manner. While some in my audience seemed reasonable and open to further consideration of my findings, a number reacted in what I thought to be a strange manner. They appeared to assume that I had been brainwashed (or something akin to it) during my visit. The incongruity of this reaction did not dawn on me until some time later: according to this reasoning, the ones who had not been to Crossroads were more trustworthy than an eyewitness!

I have encountered a somewhat similar reaction among disciples (usually leaders) who trust their own perceptions too much. When I gave my side of a situation that I had been involved in as an advisor, they discounted it, even though they had not been with me there. From a distance, they trusted themselves more than the person who was an eyewitness! Most often, the one who was not there fears that the person who was there was swayed by sentimentality toward those he was working with. Of course this is possible. All of us can become sentimental and not see things clearly. But anyone who trusts his perception to the point that he summarily dismisses the opinion of another who was much more closely involved in a situation— without really being open to that opinion—is neither very humble nor very wise. Asking questions about sentimentality is good, but a prideful assumption without such questioning is Biblically wrong.

One final application of the principle of hearing both sides is likely the most potentially dangerous to the kingdom. Those who have been hurt by someone in the kingdom and have not worked through the hurt to the point of forgiveness and resolution will become bitter. Then, once they are full of bad attitudes toward others in the church, usually leaders, they become magnets, attracting to themselves others with similar unresolved conflicts and bitterness. They begin to assume that the church is absolutely full of such "mistreatment" (their sides of the stories), and at this point, anyone with a tale of woe is heard, believed and sympathized with—even though only one side is being heard! The Old Testament story of Absalom provides a wake-up call for us. Those with unresolved hurts who talk with others with similar hurts will ultimately go the way of Absalom, whether they understand this principle or not. It is dangerous.

Many years ago, before coming to Boston, I began leading a church whose top leader before me had been reputedly harsh and overbearing. When I arrived, I was older than he and had come from a different background. People perceived that I would be easy to persuade about their mistreatment by leaders, since they knew I was made aware of the mistakes and sins of the former leader. As each came to me with complaints toward present leaders at different levels, I always listened carefully, but then arranged for the three of us to sit down with each other so that I could hear both sides. Even though their stories in isolation sounded quite plausible, I was amazed at how often the leader was not in fact the one at fault. When you hear only one side of the story, it may sound one hundred percent believable, but only until you hear both sides— preferably together—can you know what the truth really is.

Do people get hurt by others in the kingdom? Of course. This is why God gave us a double indemnity insurance policy against unresolved conflicts in Matthew 5:23-24 and Matthew 18:15-17. If we do not work hard until repentance, forgiveness and reconciliation are produced, we are not behaving as disciples of Jesus, and God will resist us. But keep in mind that much of this process involves all parties—sinner, sinned against and facilitator—hearing both sides of the story. This is the way of God for his children.

Let's keep learning how to apply our Proverbs principle. It is one of the most fundamental passages about relationships in the Bible. Knowing one side of any story is only one side—and it may not be the right side! Take the time and exercise the self-control to become a truly wise person. Get the big picture before reaching conclusions, saving yourself and others from the kinds of misunderstandings that can produce relational rifts.

To Help You Focus

1. How do you feel when someone makes judgments of you without showing interest in fully hearing your side of the story?

2. Which application of Proverbs 18:17 most applies to you? How can you use this principle to reconcile a current rift between you and someone you are in conflict with or have funny feelings toward?

3. Think back to a particular time when you judged a situation or person unfairly—i.e. without hearing his or her side. What happened? How did you eventually resolve it? How then did you feel about your quick judgment?

3
Buy Now and Pay Later

> Do not be deceived: God cannot be mocked. A
> man reaps what he sows. The one who sows to
> please his sinful nature, from that nature will
> reap destruction; the one who sows to please
> the Spirit, from the Spirit will reap eternal life.
> Let us not become weary in doing good, for at
> the proper time we will reap a harvest if we do
> not give up.
>
> Galatians 6:7-9

Our modern American credit system is a reflection of our selfish mind-set of "buy now and pay later." It is ingrained in our thinking. It may have taken our parents decades to acquire certain things, but we want them overnight and have found a way to get them: just use one of those little plastic cards. We grapple for the quick route to material success and "charge it," only to discover later that the interest rates rob us of the joy of the possessions.

When I was a young married man, I wanted to buy a certain fishing boat. I talked to an older, wiser friend about it and gave him my plethora of perfectly good reasons for why I should make the purchase. After listening carefully (and knowing that I did not really need it and could not really afford it), he replied sardonically, "Sure, go ahead and buy it. You owe it to yourself!" Wow, that stung. But I knew he was right. I had allowed my selfishness to motivate me to want to take shortcuts.

Satan surely invented this mind-set, for it is virtually identical to his temptations to draw us into sin—sin now and pay later. We want instant gratification without having to pay the price, but pay we will. Proverbs 16:25 states,

> "There is a way that seems right to a man,
>   but in the end it leads to death."

The truly valuable things in life are not painlessly and easily obtained. We reap a harvest of righteousness only after sowing, watering and weeding our own characters. The writer of Hebrews put it this way:

> No discipline seems pleasant at the time, but pain-
> ful. Later on, however, it produces a harvest of
> righteousness and peace for those who have been
> trained by it. (Hebrews 12:11)

God's way is not short-term; it is long-term. Satan says to sin now and pay later, not bothering to inform us that we will pay through the nose the high interest rates of sin. God, on the other hand, says to pay up front and gain big dividends later. Righteousness is an investment of life—our own lives—and there really are no valid shortcuts.

Perseverance is one of the most essential qualities for a disciple. We are guaranteed a harvest, but only if we do not give up. I once had a wall plaque with these words on it:

> On the plains of hesitation lie the blackened bones of countless millions, who at the very dawn of victory, sat down to rest and resting, died.

Character is not infused into babies at birth. It is built day by day, inch by inch, challenge by challenge. Without perseverance through the hard times, we do not grow. (Read carefully Romans 5:1-5, James 1:2-4 and Hebrews 12:5-14.) Anyone who holds on to God and does what he asks will ultimately come out well, no matter the sizes of the obstacles in his or her path.

The only way to lose the Christian battle is to give up the fight. Wyndham Shaw, a fellow elder, once said that perhaps our finest way of saying "I love you" to God is to simply stay in the arena—especially when the pain is great and the answers are few. After all, what is the definition of a friend, if not one who sticks by you through thick and thin? Are you God's friend? Can he count on you in the hard times or only when he gives you what you want?

I love to see baptisms, to see people embrace the new birth and the new life. They need to change, and as they go through the conversion process, many changes take place in possibly a very short time. They have a change of mind and believe in God and the Bible. They have a change of heart as they fall in love with Jesus. They have a change of will as they count the cost and repent. And to the degree that they repent, they experience a change in direction, in behavior. While it is true that many changes can occur in a brief span of time through repentance, deeper character changes take much longer. Some changes result from one's initial repentance and some from Christian growth. Unless new disciples understand the difference, they can be scared and frustrated about their new lives in Christ.

Not too long ago, I studied the Scriptures with a man for a period of several months. He seemed to understand the lessons quite well and fairly quickly affirmed his desire to be baptized into Christ. Yet more and more time passed, and he was not able to go forward. His relationship with his performance-oriented father had left its mark on him. He never felt that he knew enough or would be able to do enough to be a good disciple, so he procrastinated for weeks before he decided that he did want to be a disciple. Among other things, he had to be helped to see that some changes result from the initial decision to repent and some from continued repentance.

Our decision to repent before baptism is a decision to devote our lives to Jesus for as long as we live. The things that we know are wrong, we must quit doing; the things that we know are right, we must start doing. We also decide that we will begin or cease to practice all that we *later learn* to be right or wrong. Beyond this, our hearts must be committed to becoming as much like Jesus as possible, no matter what or how long it takes. God is not in the zapping business (as in "Zap, you're changed!"). He expects us to put his principles into practice consistently until our characters are different (Hebrews 5:14). He requires a time of sowing and reaping, most likely because it both tests and develops our dependence on him.

When God created the universe, each member of Deity had a part. The Father had the plan, the eternal *logos* (Jesus) was the agent of creation (John 1:1-3), and the Spirit brought the creation into perfection (Genesis 1). Many Biblical scholars think that this process took place over a long period of time, which is not surprising, since time means nothing to God. A parallel may be seen with the church. The Father was the designer, the Son was the agent in his personal ministry and death, and the Spirit came on Pentecost to begin bringing everything to completion. Keep in mind that this final stage took awhile, for it was years before the Gentiles were ushered in and the Biblical record complete. Now apply the same principle to the maturing process that God uses for us as individuals. It is a process that takes time, and it is much more gradual than we all at times wish. However, the perseverance de-manded on our parts provides the greatest of opportunities to demonstrate true faith. Faith shines brightest when tested in the greatest ways.

Patience is a quality that is highly esteemed by God. It is one of his characteristics and therefore, a fruit of the Spirit (Galatians 5:22). To consistently exhibit patience, two things are required. One, we must learn to control our selfish emotions. We want what we want, and we want it now! This is a childish approach to life, but many adults have not matured out of this self-focused way of thinking and feeling. Hence, denying self in order to carry the cross means that we deny selfish emotions. Jesus did this at Gethsemane even though he was facing death. To be his followers, we must do the same. Spiritual babies throw tantrums, at least inwardly, and they are often tempted to take their toys and go home (in other words, to give up).

Two, we must have a heart full of trust in God. Patience means trusting that God will take care of everything that happens in our lives. All things do work together for good in order for us to become more and more like Jesus. Romans 8:28 cannot be understood without Romans 8:29. We always know what we want, but God always knows what we need. If we trust that God is working daily in our lives, then each day is an adventure—not a bundle of pressure and anxiety.

Are we willing to relax and let God run our lives? Or will we remain on the "buy now and pay later" track? If the latter, we will eventually bring serious spiritual calamities on ourselves and on those close to us. May God grant us the patience and perseverance that is characterized by a childlike trust in him. Then the psalmist's words in Psalm 131:2 will be true of us:

> But I have stilled and quieted my soul;
>   like a weaned child with its mother,
>   like a weaned child is my soul within me.

To Help You Focus

1. How are you most tempted to cut corners in your spiritual life?

2. Who in your life has taught you the most about perseverance and what specifically have you learned from him or her?

3. In regard to what matter do you most need patience? How will walking close to God help you to have it?

The Easy Way Out

> "And I'll say to myself, 'You have plenty of good things laid up for many years. Take life easy; eat, drink and be merry.'"
>
> Luke 12:19

Taking the easy way out is about as normal as breathing. We are enamored with laborsaving devices. I have always liked watches and have often bought those having the latest technology. The one I have now downloads directly from my computer and holds 150 names and phone numbers. However, I recall a new type of watch that came on the market years ago that I would not buy. It was called an LED (light-emitting diode) watch, and instead of having the traditional hands pointing to numbers, the face was blank until you pushed a button that caused the LED to light up with digital numbers (usually red or turquoise). This type was briefly very popular, but I knew they would not last in America. As much as we love pushing buttons to set a dishwasher or clothes dryer in motion, we would never go from doing *nothing* (simply looking at the hands on a watch) to pushing a button. That would seem, well, un-American! I waited for the LCD (lead crystal display) model that keeps the numbers visible at all times. This feature, in combination with the many other features available on this type of watch, makes sense to me.

Spiritually speaking, God's program with each of his children is to mold us more and more into the image of his Son. It is wonderfully true that "in all things God works for the good of those who love him" (Romans 8:28), but the purpose of his work is that "those God foreknew he also predestined to be conformed to the likeness of his Son" (Romans 8:29). Ease of life was never God's intention for his creatures. Yes, Jesus' yoke is easy because it fits us so well, and yet, at the heart of Jesus' message is the call to take up the cross daily. Those looking for something without challenge or pain, need not apply.

A desire for taking the easy way out manifests itself in many ways. For example, we want medicine to alleviate aches and pains in situations that would be better solved by prevention, perhaps through nutrition and exercise. We are quick to self-diagnose our physical problems as chronic fatigue or some similar malady, thereby rationalizing away our lethargic natures, when the problems may be emotional, not physical, to start with.[1] Similarly, some with persistent sin problems are quick to question their original baptism and to think that another baptism would solve their difficulties. However, only repentance based on deep and abiding convictions will produce change— before or after baptism. We need all the help we can get

---

[1] I am not referring to those who have been diagnosed by a physician. Medical opinion is agreed that such a condition indeed exists and is a very frustrating disease to those who have it, a frustration often exacerbated by having the uninformed discount the reality of their condition.

from every source, including the Holy Spirit who indwells Christians at baptism (Acts 2:38), but we will never change and remain changed unless we deny self daily. There are simply no shortcuts.

Repentance can be induced by God in two basic ways: his kindness (Romans 2:4) or his discipline (Hebrews 12:5-11). I always try to choose the former! When we do not respond to God's grace, he will use whatever means necessary to motivate us to repent. Character change at the deepest level almost always comes by our traveling the *Via Dolorosa*, the "way of suffering." According to passages like Romans 5:1-5 and James 1:2-4, character change only comes by persevering through suffering. Continuing to persevere brings a maturity that yields hope for the future. Having a track record of hanging in during the rough times begets endurance for future trials. A remarkable passage along these lines is Hebrews 5:7-10, which reads:

> During the days of Jesus' life on earth, he offered up prayers and petitions with loud cries and tears to the one who could save him from death, and he was heard because of his reverent submission. Although he was a son, he learned obedience from what he suffered and, once made perfect, he became the source of eternal salvation for all who obey him and was designated by God to be high priest in the order of Melchizedek.

Jesus was perfect in his sinlessness, but *made perfect* for his high priestly role only by learning through his suffering. This is an incredible statement, is it not? Jesus, the

God-man, had to suffer to be matured for his role on our behalf. If he had to suffer to be trained, need we wonder if we must suffer to refine our characters? The question for us is not *if*, but only when and how much.

Being a disciple is not easy, nor was it designed to be. Growth comes at a cost, and the greater the gain in spirituality, the larger the price tag. This explains much of why the Bible puts such a premium on age. Only with the passing of years can we reach certain levels of spiritual depth. It is somewhat an issue of experience, but perhaps more an issue of enduring the kinds of pain that force our souls and compassion to expand.

John the apostle, in his early years as a "Son of Thunder" (Mark 3:17), may have exhibited a zeal much admired by the "young guns" among his associates, but God was far from finished with him at that point. He was to become the old "apostle of love," who with years of life under his belt, understood the greatest two commands (Matthew 22:36-40) far better than he ever could have as a young zealot. The Bible is quite clear on the matter: Spiritual zeal is not equal to spiritual maturity, although spiritual maturity will include spiritual zeal (Romans 12:11).

Sometimes we can be spiritual "slow learners," avoiding the normal pains that produce growth until we finally hit bottom and have nowhere to look but up. The path to the bottom likely is found in one of two main ways. One, we gradually slip into weakness without the appearance of overt sin in our lives. Hitting bottom without obvious sin may also occur when big emotional hits come, such as family, financial or health problems—or worse, the death of a loved one. The depressed state is not caused by out-and-out rebellion or "big" sins (other than not dealing with the challenges in a spiritual way). It is simply a gradual weakening through unrecognized sin which is not dealt with specifically.

Two, we may hit bottom emotionally because of a hidden sin that is not brought out into the open and repented of, and the built-in consequences of the sin ultimately take their toll on us.

Once people become this depressed and hopeless—through either avenue—their symptoms are the same. However, the treatment is different, depending on the cause of their downward spiral. The route taken to get there determines the solution. For the one who finds his strength depleted without the presence of noticeable sin, a gradual reconditioning is often an adequate cure. Obviously, this person needs to take responsibility for allowing the drifting to have occurred. As with those who lose physical conditioning, they need to choose a regimen of spiritual reconditioning. If they start doing what is necessary, they should regain their strength in a gradual but consistent manner. If this approach does not work, it probably indicates that the problem is more related to the following case.

For the one who brought the hopelessness on himself because of flagrant sin, the solution is more radical. To make the physical parallel, an operation is required, followed by

changing the lifestyle to avoid a return to the same malady—
like bypass surgery followed by a change in diet, exercise
and quitting smoking. Note that those with advanced arterial
blockage cannot solve the problem by the new lifestyle
alone, but must undergo some painful surgery. Spiritually,
people in this category must reach a deep state of brokenness, which is painful. No other route will do. They must
understand their sin and develop a deep conviction about
it before their repentance can be complete. Helpful Biblical
remedies include a study of pride and related items in the
book of Proverbs; studying the subject of divine discipline
in such passages as Hebrews 12:5-17; and a study of Jacob's
wrestling match with God (Genesis 32:22-32) which shows
the need to really strive for brokenness. Understanding the
radical nature of repentance and how it manifests itself will
be aided by a contemplative study of 2 Corinthians 7:8-11
and James 4:1-8.

Sentimentality is a spiritual blight in any of its forms, but
it is most dangerous when exercised in our own behalf. It
keeps us away from the Surgeon's expert scalpel. God is
full of love, to be sure, but he is absolutely devoid of
sentimentality. He will give us what we need instead of
what we think we need—because he loves us. Since our
assessment of what our needs are will often differ significantly from his, we had better be prepared for experiences
that do not feel like love. God is determined to raise us up
into righteous maturity in spite of our temporary weeping
and wailing when the rod of discipline is applied. The more

and sooner we cooperate, the quicker the trials we are facing may end—so cooperate!

It's important to understand how spiritual growth occurs at the deeper level, and it's far more important to embrace it with appreciation of God and of the process he uses. Do you want to be joyful and fulfilled? Then become spiritually mature. Do you really want to be mature? Then pray that God will do whatever it takes to help you become increasingly like his Son.

> Those who sow in tears
> will reap with songs of joy.
> He who goes out weeping,
> carrying seed to sow,
> will return with songs of joy,
> carrying sheaves with him. (Psalm 126:5-6)

Never will this principle be more applicable than when the sheaves of the harvest are those of your own personal growth. Reject the temptation to desire (and take!) the easy way out. Remember Proverbs 14:12,

> There is a way that seems right to a man,
> but in the end it leads to death.

Pursue spirituality, complete with its necessary challenges, for in the end it leads to God.

To Help You Focus

1. Think about your past. Has it led you to have a positive or negative view of growth pains? (For example, an athlete may have a better grasp of the value of pain.)

2. How does your attitude toward God's training need to change?

3. What current situations are you facing that God may be trying to use to mold your character? In what ways are you trying to find an easy way out? What will submission to God mean?

5 Emotions and Spirituality

> During the days of Jesus' life on earth, he
> offered up prayers and petitions with loud
> cries and tears to the one who could save him
> from death, and he was heard because of his
> reverent submission.
>
> Hebrews 5:7

Recently my son (by marriage to our daughter) shared with me a statement made by a younger disciple to the man who was marrying his sister. He said, "You are my hero because you are one of the few I have seen who could be emotional and doing well spiritually at the same time." His comment demonstrates that someone described as emotional is usually emotionally out of control (as in, "Oh, he is just being emotional again"). Our emotions can easily lead us to be unspiritual and damaging to ourselves and others. Being an emotionally based person myself, I understand the challenges. After doing or saying something stupid in a bad emotional state, I have wished that I could have an "emotionectomy"!

Emotions are God-given and intended to be a blessing to us and to others around us. But because they are often not kept under the umbrella of self-control, they can be negatively used, and therefore, negatively viewed. Many men and some women tend to be afraid of emotions and think that showing them is a weakness. Likely, a part of the reason they feel this way is because they have borne the brunt of consequences from emotions gone awry. However, another part of the equation is pride. In our culture, big boys should not cry, and for those who accept this premise, the idea of men crying ranks right up there with cowardice and other unsavory qualities.

The truth is that we are made with emotions because God has emotions. How we view and use them is the real issue. Those who thwart their emotions, for whatever reason, are not like Jesus. Further, they are, for the most part, prideful cowards, afraid of showing their true feelings. Some disciples refuse to get open and honest with their hurt emotions. Again, they are both afraid and prideful. Perhaps they are open with some types of people, but closed with other types. For example, they may only be honest with those under them in spiritual maturity or leadership, or they may only be real with those over them. Mark it down, if we are not characterized by openness with all types of people, we are the ones who are weak, however effective we may be at covering up our emotions with a thin facade. Please, for your own good, force yourself to be open and honest until it develops into a righteous habit!

We may also be reserved in expressing positive emotions, especially in giving compliments and sharing our love and appreciation verbally. This failure is based less on fear and more on pride. We just somehow have difficulty saying, "I love you," or "I need you," which is a shame. If people need anything from others, it is to be told how much they mean to them. In times of crisis, we usually get past our emotional blockage and express ourselves much better. I have noticed that times of grief bring out this expressive side of us, but verbal statements of love are too important to reserve for funerals. Let's deal with both our fears and pride and learn to be more like God, who opens wide his heart to us time after time in the Bible.

Returning to the subject of the potentially negative impact of emotions, one of the most important lessons that we must learn is that negative emotions are not to be trusted. They may be real and they may be strong, but they are likely not very accurate. Once I was sharing with a group of ministry staff people the sinful tendency to build a case in our own minds about a person or a situation and to play the negative scene over and over until it seems absolutely true. One brother told me that he doesn't play negative scenes over and over—he plays whole movies! In other words, he assumes many things and keeps them inside until the negative movie is complete and the worst-case scenario seems inevitable. How tragic! But mark this down: Unless you allow others to break into your closed system of reasoning, the illogical will continue to seem perfectly logical.

Some married couples keep such emotionally damaging assumptions between themselves, and they feed off each other's negativity until Satan's whirlpool pulls them under the surface of reality and truth. For God's sake, quit allowing the devil to have his way with your emotions. Get open, get help, and quit wallowing in your pigpen of assumption and illusion. Emotions are too often used by Satan in an amazingly damaging way, but God wants to use them in an amazingly helpful way. When they begin to go in a negative direction, opening and getting help will allow you to gain perspective on your situation.

Perceptions can be mistaken. When negative emotions are connected to them, they are nearly always mistaken. When these perceptions deal with anything close to your heart, tread carefully. I trust my perception about others pretty well. After years of experience working with great numbers and types of people, my insights into people are normally reasonably accurate. However, when I am talking about perceptions of myself and those close to me, especially family, my emotions can cloud the picture considerably. Our strong human tendency is to trust our emotions most exactly when we should trust them least. The higher the stakes of our choices, the more emotions are involved—and the more emotions are involved, the less likely we are to make correct choices. Hence, we need to allow others to have input into our perceptions and decisions.

Wyndham Shaw and I, as elders who have worked together for years, have learned some valuable lessons along these lines. If either one of us gets emotionally "hooked" in some setting, we tell the other what we are feeling and then ask for help in developing the right perspective. If either of us tells the other that he is off base, we quickly accept the input as being accurate. We are all too aware that anything of a personal nature tends to arouse negative emotions and taint our perceptions. How much do you trust your perception about yourself or your family? True spirituality takes into account the need to have others help us with perceptions when our emotions are not positive.

I have met some people who are so skewed in their perspectives of themselves that unless they are open to accepting others' evaluations of them, they cannot survive emotionally or spiritually for long. Sadly, the more skewed they are, the less likely they are to accept the needed input. For the ones who do, they ultimately develop a good early warning system to help them stay out of the pit of trusting negative emotions about themselves. For the ones who do not, they are doomed to stay locked in their illogical lines of reasoning and will remain in emotional misery until they decide to accept the evaluations of others as being more accurate than their own.

Emotions, viewed and used correctly, are absolutely necessary to us if we are serious about imitating Jesus. I know that he cried regularly (Hebrews 5:7), and I have to believe that he laughed regularly. (Where do you think we got our sense of humor?) He was open about his disappointments (Luke 19:41-44) and about his struggles (Matthew 26:36-46). He was also expressive of his love for others, his need for others and his excitement about what God was doing in their lives.

Babies are born emotionally based, and expressing their true feelings is not a problem for them! Only with time and false training do they develop emotional constipation. It is time to change the trend, for spiritual qualities like joy are, by definition, emotional in nature. Truly inspirational people are emotional people, and their emotions are expressed in transparent ways. Thank God for those who are both emotionally based and spiritually strong at the same time! It may be a difficult balance to attain, but then, true spirituality is never easily obtained nor maintained. May God help us to get to that pinnacle, for when we do, our own happiness and our impact on others will be multiplied greatly. We can be spiritual and emotional at the same time. It is the way of Jesus—imitate him.

To Help You Focus

1. Do you know yourself well? Do you understand how you naturally are when it comes to emotions? Do you know the ways you are tempted to either stuff emotions or let them loose in wrong ways?

2. Who are you allowing into your heart to help you see how to handle your emotions in spiritually productive ways?

3. Do a careful study of these passages about tears in the lives of the spiritually minded: Acts 20:19, 20:31; 2 Corinthians 2:4; Philippians 3:18; 2 Timothy 1:4; Hebrews 5:7; and Hebrews 12:17. How do these passages change your thinking?

In Touch and Out of the Pit

> To you, O Lord, I called;
>> to the Lord I cried for mercy:
> "What gain is there in my destruction,
>> in my going down into the pit?
> Will the dust praise you?
>> Will it proclaim your faithfulness?
> Hear, O Lord, and be merciful to me;
>> O Lord, be my help."
>
> Psalm 30:8-10

A year ago, my wife and I went off for a few days to enjoy a marriage getaway. Both of us had been quite busy beforehand and needed some rest, and due to our schedule, we also needed some time to rekindle our relationship. No sooner had we arrived at the little bed-and-breakfast than we had one of our worst "bumps" of the year. Expectations were dashed, feelings were hurt and sins were committed (mostly by me). What happened? How did we get so far off track so fast? Good questions, these, and strangely, it took me a few days to come up with the answer. Normally, I am very in touch with my emotions and can tell quickly what is bothering me when I am upset or down in spirit. But in this situation, I really did not have much of a clue.

I went for a long prayer walk and asked God to help me get in touch with what was in my heart, but the picture remained unclear. Finally, I did what my wife often does: I wrote out my feelings in detail—for about two hours on my laptop computer. Our emotions can be "out there" until we distill them. Talking condenses the scattered thoughts into a more specific form, but then writing focuses them even further into a much more compact form. At this juncture, we usually can begin to make sense of the confusion and get in touch with the pain inside. After my time of writing, I came to understand the several strands of tension and anxiety that had built up in my heart. I shared what I wrote with Theresa. Then with it all out in the light, I felt like I could get my arms around it, understand it and surrender all of it in prayer to God. It was amazing how freed up I felt after doing that!

David is a classic example of someone who controlled his emotions by pouring them out in writing and then surrendering them to God. Time after time he began a psalm with an anguished spirit, but by the end of it, he was full of faith in God's ultimate control of his life. I don't think he was simply sitting down with quill in hand to write another book of the Bible; I believe that, with his particular emotional makeup, writing was a huge part of the way he related to his heavenly Father. God then ultimately used this writing to encourage the rest of us, and further, to teach us a method of keeping on track spiritually: writing out our prayers and feelings to him.

As helpful as writing is in dealing with current emotions, it is even more important in helping us deal with our past emotions, especially if these still affect the present. Our childhood years are the most formative years, of course, and most of us will do far better in life if we understand how they affect us.

For example, I can remember talking with a young man who had negative views of women and their role in the kingdom. It seemed obvious to me that he had been hurt badly by a woman (or women) in the past, and sure enough, as I asked about it, he shared very painful memories of his mother and the terrible relationship they had had during his growing up years.

On another occasion I recall talking to a couple who were highly disturbed by any disagreement between them, to the point that they each became very hurt and shut down emotionally every time. As I asked about their parents' relationships when they were growing up, the answer was as expected: both witnessed terrible fights without any attempts at rational resolution. Yet another example was that of a wife who was filled with suspicions and distrust of her faithful husband. Once again, the questions revealed her painful memories of a father who had consistently cheated on her mother and had been extremely deceitful in hiding and then denying his unfaithfulness.

Not everyone has had a messed up past, but many of us have—in fact, probably most of us. Years back, as my wife was reading a book about dysfunctional families, she began sharing the characteristics of such families with me. Even though I had not thought of my own family in this way, I came to realize that my own childhood was spent in the midst of a very dysfunctional family. In our morally worsening world, not many families are emotionally healthy, to say nothing of being spiritually healthy. Without doubt, a number of us need to work through our pasts by writing and talking about the things that hurt us as children. The chemical recovery ministries understand this principle well, for an absolute requirement of being in this group is writing a detailed journal of your past.[1]

Let me share another example that will show some specifics about how to work through past emotional damage. A young married disciple came to me for help with his temper—in Biblical terms, "fits of rage" (Galatians 5:20). I spent one session finding out the extent of his sin and something about his childhood. Then I asked John (not his real name) to write a letter addressed to his father and older brother, the ones toward whom he held the most bitterness. The principle here is that our undealt-with hurts always result in anger and finally, bitterness. Thus, I had him write letters to the ones who hurt him most, explaining to him that he was not going to give them the letters, but only use them as a tool to help him get in touch with what he really felt. I told John to begin the letters something like this: "Dear Dad, As I think back to what life as a child was like with you, here are the things I remember most...." Our

---

[1] For much more about the Chemical Recovery ministry see *Some Sat in Darkness* (Woburn, Mass.: Discipleship Publications International, 1998).

memories contain emotions, both good and bad. Some people, in writing, discover many positive memories that they tended to forget, which helps balance out the painful ones, but for sure the latter will be uncovered.

As John wrote these two letters, he felt the emotional turmoil of being a ten-year-old again. When he first started reading his letters to me the next time we got together, his pain, steeped in anger, poured out. He felt like that little child being mistreated again, and it caused him great pain. After he had shared it all with me, I then shared from my own life, describing my father's anger, which was vented often on me and my mother—and her extreme emotional hysteria in response. My childhood was spent in an emotional hothouse, and it definitely left its mark on me. Thankfully, my father changed a lot as he grew older, and we became the closest of friends for the last twenty-five years of his life. But that did not undo the damage. I had to work that through mostly by myself, because I was not in a church then that offered much help emotionally or spiritually.

What helped me most was to think back to what my father had been through himself. My dad's father had been worse than my father was, so Dad had his own emotional baggage to bear and no example of a normal father to imitate. As I thought about this, I felt less anger toward my dad, but began feeling it toward my grandfather, who had warped my father! But then I thought, "Wait a minute! You didn't even know your great-grandfather. Maybe he was even worse—and messed up your grandfather!" The more

I reasoned along these lines, it became obvious that the only one on whom I could logically place the blame was Satan: He was behind it all. Of course, my dad, granddad and great-granddad all bear some responsibility, but expecting those in the world to act like Christians is unrealistic. Once I had developed a mature spiritual perspective, I was able to surrender every vestige of hurt and bitterness. Now I can think back with no emotional pain to specific things my father did in those early years that hurt very deeply at the time. By God's grace, I have been healed.

Sharing about my background helped John tremendously. We talked about his father and brother and what could have damaged them, for surely no one could treat a ten-year-old child like they had treated him unless they had some serious problems themselves. At the end of it all, my friend was able to give up his anger and attach adult emotions to the childhood memories. He only felt compassion for his family members who were in the grasp of Satan, and instead of being vengeful, he wanted to show them God in his life and hopefully share with them the cure that he himself had found. After writing those pain-filled, anger-drenched letters, he surrendered his pain and repented of his own sins in response.[2]

Thankfully, not everyone needs to work through emotional damage from the past. How can you tell if you should? Basically, if you have emotional issues that seem

[2] Sometimes at this point, I suggest writing another letter that is actually sent to the person(s), but this should only be done with advice of those experienced with such situations. Done correctly, these second letters, with the anger edited out, can do wonders to open much-needed lines of communication. Done incorrectly, damage will be done, so proceed only with good advice if it seems appropriate to use this option.

almost impossible to overcome, these are the best indicators. Some are able to pray and surrender and put even very damaging things behind them (without just "stuffing" their feelings). Others are like a tree growing out of the ground crooked. No matter how much you work to straighten it up, it always goes back in alignment with its root system. In that case, you must dig down to the roots, free them up and reset them at the correct angle. Like the tree, if we cannot seem to get straightened up emotionally and stay straightened up, we may well need some help realigning our roots. To help you figure out what is needed, get advice from mature leaders. Also, read "I Was Born This Way!" (chapter 12) to help you avoid the extremes at both ends of the spectrum.

No matter what may or may not be needed regarding working through your past, writing out your feelings (and expressing your faith as you do) is something I highly recommend. Peter told us, "Therefore be clear minded and self-controlled so that you can pray" (1 Peter 4:7). Clearing our minds certainly is crucial if we want to think spiritually. Writing down our feelings helps us work our way to faith.

To Help You Focus

1. Take a few minutes and write down how you felt in a recent situation which was distressing. Describe those feelings fully.

2. Now write down words of thanksgiving to God for hearing your pain or frustration.

3. Next write down, addressing it to God, what you know he has said that applies to this situation.

4. What do you think about keeping a journal of such thoughts? Will you commit to do it for the next month?

7 Ambition—from God or Satan?

> It is true that some preach Christ out of envy and rivalry, but others out of goodwill. The latter do so in love, knowing that I am put here for the defense of the gospel. The former preach Christ out of selfish ambition, not sincerely, supposing that they can stir up trouble for me while I am in chains. But what does it matter? The important thing is that in every way, whether from false motives or true, Christ is preached. And because of this I rejoice.
>
> Philippians 1:15-18

Ambition is a much-admired quality in our world. Biblically, the word "ambition" is neutral. It can be positive (as in Romans 15:20 and 1 Thessalonians 4:11) or negative (as in the text above and Galatians 5:20), depending on the motives behind it. If you use the New International Version of the Bible, you will often find that the word "selfish" is connected with the word "ambition." If our ambition is selfish, it is sinful. Unselfish ambition is spiritual. However, the difference between the two is much more difficult to distinguish than we often realize.

As disciples, we can mistakenly assume that selfish ambition is confined to worldly pursuits. In other words, if my ambition is to get rich or to become president, it is worldly and therefore selfish. But our desires to accomplish purely spiritual ends can just as easily qualify as selfish ambition. Jesus' interaction with the apostles James and John, described in Matthew 20:20-28, demonstrates the point clearly. Prompted by an ambitious mother, the two requested leadership seats on Jesus' right and left. The other apostles heard about the request and were indignant. They were not righteously indignant over the brothers' sin—they wanted their own shot at top leadership slots. They were desirous of spiritual leadership, which can be a very good thing, but their motives rendered the desire sinful.

Ambition in the kingdom can be a powerful tool for God or for Satan. But keep in mind always that spiritual goals do not make ambitions spiritual. We often want right things for wrong reasons. Several inherent dangers regarding ambitions must be avoided, which means that we need to understand these dangers well.

One danger is that we can become far too focused on positional goals in the church and become unspiritual in the process. Some have set their hearts on leadership positions that are frankly beyond the scope of their spiritual gifts. They are set up for disappointment and disillusionment in God, themselves and the kingdom. Those who set their hearts on goals that they do not and cannot reach will feel like failures and second-class citizens. I am far more comfortable with living by what I call the "Joseph principle." Surely his earlier dreams had taken a major hit, and at this stage, he likely had no idea that he could be the second in command of the greatest nation on earth. He was a slave and a prisoner for thirteen years. The only ambition that seemed possible for him was that of serving and trusting God to the best of his ability on a daily basis. But because that was his heart, God was able to exalt him beyond his wildest dreams. What if each of us lived each day with one thought in mind: to be as much like Jesus as possible? Do you really think that the church would be short on leaders?

Another danger is found in a similar realm, that of wanting to be excellent in the world's eyes through sports, entertainment, academics or business endeavors—with very mixed motives. Surely we want to do our best at whatever we are doing, as Colossians 3:23 instructs: "Whatever you do, work at it with all your heart, as working for the Lord, not for men." Doing everything excellently allows us to better influence others, all else being equal. The key is that we need to do it *for the Lord*, not for self or others through tainted motives. It is easy to enjoy the praise of men for such achievements, if we are not very careful. Being in the limelight is very appealing in many ways.

Probably my biggest concern along these lines is how we motivate our children. If our children have the talent and the spirituality to handle the pressures of being in the public's eye for their achievements, well and good. But if they do not, undue pressure for such achievements will damage them in ways we will not understand fully until they are adults. I remember one minister expressing frustration with his child because the child did not have "kingdom dreams." Realizing that the child in question had only average ability, I hurt for the pain of failure and disapproval the child likely felt from a well-meaning but overzealous parent. I did try to help him see this subtle but damaging mistake.

Our expectations for our children to excel in sports or academics or in the ministry can be unrealistic for them. Proverbs 22:6 says to "train a child in the way *he* should go," (emphasis added). If the emphasis falls here where I suspect it does, this would mean for the parent to figure out which talents and abilities are unique to each child and train them accordingly—avoiding the tendency of trying to force them into molds they don't fit into.

Parents, as an older and hopefully wiser man, I am trying to get your attention here. Being the best we can be is Biblical and right; pushing someone to be what he or she was not designed to be is wrong and damaging. Development of a spiritual character is far more important than accomplishments in other realms. Let's be very careful on this one and get plenty of advice. It will not only save us from heartaches; it will keep some children from leaving the church as they grow older.

A third danger in channeling our ambition comes in allowing secondary motivations to become primary motivations. To help you understand what this means, let me share with you an illustration from my life some years ago. I was reasonably well-known in my former circle of churches and felt comfortable speaking to audiences of whatever size. But somehow I felt that I did enjoy the limelight in the wrong way.

I was invited to deliver a keynote speech at a campus ministry seminar as a virtual unknown in that group. I felt very insecure as I overheard people looking at the program and saying, "Gordon Ferguson—who is that?" Since I didn't speak until near the end of the seminar, I actually heard such statements a number of times. After I spoke (and my insecurities prompted me to speak well), everyone knew who I was and seemed reasonably impressed. But I did not feel good at all about my response and had to ask the question of why I was doing what I was doing. Was I more concerned with impressing men or God?

As I wrestled with those concerns, I took a one-year hiatus from speaking outside of my home congregation, refusing all such requests. I prayed a lot, asking God to help me understand my heart and my motivations. I also asked advice of mature spiritual leaders. One of them gave me some input that I never forgot. He really thought that my primary motivation was righteous and that I wanted to serve God and people. But he suggested that I might have some secondary motivations that were mixed. His insights left me feeling better, which allowed me to keep serving with a clear conscience. But they also motivated me to keep purifying my ambitions. Through the years, they have become much purer. I believe that most of us have a combination of motives that are often mixed. Some important lessons about the relationship between primary and secondary motivations are in order.

One such lesson is that problems develop when secondary motivations become the primary ones. Examples of this principle abound. We should work hard at our careers, but why—to glorify God or to make money? We need the money to support our families, but if that secondary motive becomes primary, we have a spiritual problem. Jacob worked for seven years to earn the right to marry Rachel. He was pretty obvious about at least one motive for marriage as he approached her father: "Then Jacob said to Laban, 'Give me my wife. My time is completed, and I want to lie with her'" (Genesis 29:21). Now most will admit that sexual relations in marriage are very special and very important, but if sex is the primary motivation for marriage, heartache lies only a short distance down the nuptial road. What is our primary motivation for being baptized into Christ— to dedicate the rest of our lives to being followers and imitators of Jesus or to find peace in our lives? All of these secondary motivations are fine in their place, but if they become the primary motivations, spiritual maladies always ensue.

Now consider a more sensitive example. The greatest command in the Bible is to love God with all of our hearts, souls, minds and strength (Matthew 22:36-38, Mark 12:28-31). Compared to this command, all other commands are secondary. This includes very important things like evangelism goals, learning the facts of the Bible, being disciplined, being discipled and giving our money—to name but a few. If we allow a focus on accomplishments to supercede our focus on knowing and loving God, we can exalt kingdom success (by whatever definition) over God, thus making *it* our god. Baptism and growth goals have their place, but we can go overboard on a numbers focus. The book of Acts has numerous reports of growth, but in only two cases are specific numbers mentioned. Acts 2:41 informs us that "about three thousand" were baptized, and Acts 4:4 says, "the number of men grew to about five thousand." Other than these two accounts, no other New Testament passages state specific growth numbers.

When I wrote *Revolution!*, an exposition on the book of Acts, I was struck with the fact that the emphasis in preaching was clearly on the subject of Deity (God, Christ and the Holy Spirit). Further, in studying the nature of the New Testament letters, the focus was twofold: Deity and relationships in the church. Should that surprise us? Jesus said in John 12:32, "But I, when I am lifted up from the earth, will draw all men to myself." You would therefore expect the message of the early church to focus largely on the cross, and Paul indicates precisely this truth in 1 Corinthians 2:2: "For I resolved to know nothing while I was with you except Jesus Christ and him crucified." In our preaching, is Jesus the agenda or the addenda?

The focus on relationships in the church is explained by passages like the familiar John 13:34-35.

"A new command I give you: Love one another. As I have loved you, so you must love one another. By this all men will know that you are my disciples, if you love one another."

Love for God must lead to loving his children in a deep, abiding way. The focus in Acts and the letters was on Deity and Christian relationships, not on numbers and growth per se. Yet, the first century church grew amazingly. It is not unreasonable to assume that evangelism was a result of this focus. When people are excited about God, growing in their knowledge of him and loving the family of God, evangelism becomes a sharing of good news rather than simply a spiritual obligation or a feverish attempt to reach a numerical goal.

Why are new converts normally more effective in evangelism than those who are more mature? Is it a question of having more fresh contacts, or of having a fresher heart? They may have the former, but I suspect the real reason is found in the latter. I am convinced that we must examine our motivations and approaches to discover just why we do what we do. Church growth is God's plan and certainly expected by him, make no mistake about that; but sustaining it for the long term is the deeper issue. If our primary motivation is to love God and love his people, we will grow. But to be perfectly clear on the matter, unless this love is the focus of our teaching and preaching, it will not be our primary motivation.

Ambition—from God or Satan? That is the question. Kingdom success by any man's definition is not the Biblical definition of what our primary motivation and focus should be. Let's keep our minds and hearts open, keep digging deeply in the Bible and trust God to help us keep ambition in its proper place.

To Help You Focus

1. What are your three greatest ambitions at this point in your life?

2. What have you done to test them to see if they are spiritual or worldly?

3. Do you trust your own heart to make these judgments, or do you need help? Whose help do you need?

8 Money—the Root of All Evil?

> People who want to get rich fall into temptation and a trap and into many foolish and harmful desires that plunge men into ruin and destruction. For the love of money is a root of all kinds of evil. Some people, eager for money, have wandered from the faith and pierced themselves with many griefs.
>
> 1 Timothy 6:9-10

How many times have I heard people say that money is the root of all evil? It is a common misconception, partially because money and evil are characteristically connected. However, the Bible warns against the *love of* money rather than against money itself. Such love is connected with a host of other sins, including greed, envy, jealousy, anxiety, stealing and ingratitude. Materialism is an insidious spiritual malady, but materialism is not always easy to define.

For many of us, materialism is what people are guilty of who have more material blessings than we! Before I had two cars, the materialistic folk were the ones who did. While I was still renting a house, the materialistic were home owners. Before I had a savings or retirement account, those who did were viewed as materialistic and lacking true faith in the providence of God. Of course, once I had these things, the bar of determining materialism was raised to exclude me and include those with slightly more blessings than I. We get the point, don't we? Having been raised in a blue-collar family, I was envious and suspicious of those who "had money" (meaning more than we did). Through the years, extricating myself from distorted thinking about money has been a long and arduous process, and yes, still probably an incomplete one. But thankfully, I have made much progress. We simply must develop a spiritual perspective regarding money, for although we cannot live without it, we can easily be cursed by it.

Solomon, himself a rich man, had great insights into the blessings and curses of money. In Ecclesiastes 5, he talked about both sides of this coin. First, verses 10-12:

> Whoever loves money never has money enough;
> whoever loves wealth is never satisfied with
> his income.
> This too is meaningless.
> As goods increase,
> so do those who consume them.
> And what benefit are they to the owner
> except to feast his eyes on them?
> The sleep of a laborer is sweet,
> whether he eats little or much,
> but the abundance of a rich man
> permits him no sleep.

Then in verses 18-20, he shows the power of spiritual thinking regarding money.

> Then I realized that it is good and proper for a man to eat and drink, and to find satisfaction in his toilsome labor under the sun during the few days of life God has given him—for this is his lot. Moreover, when God gives any man wealth and possessions, and enables him to enjoy them, to accept his lot and be happy in his work—this is a gift of God. He seldom reflects on the days of his life, because God keeps him occupied with gladness of heart.

Did you get the point that God can give us money and enable us to enjoy it without sin? The real issue is not whether we have money, but how we obtain it, view it and use it.

Years ago, when I began really grasping the magnitude of the Great Commission and what it would take monetarily, I started praying that we would convert more truly rich people. It is no surprise that God chose America as the place to raise up our movement. We have the most money and therefore the most potential to send out mission teams all over the world. Americans are not necessarily more spiritually minded, but we definitely are more financially endowed. Hence, God has used American churches to fund mission work in a grand way. But we have only just begun to reach the six billion inhabitants of Planet Earth, and it will take huge amounts of money to finish the task.

In one sense, of course, God doesn't need either our money or us. He owns everything. But he did provide the plan to evangelize that demands both. Praise God that I see those earlier prayers for rich people in the kingdom being answered! Most of the ones I know in this category were not rich when converted, but were blessed with riches after conversion. Romans 12:8 describes a "gift" of giving, which would include both the ability to make money and the heart to give it generously. I pray that we have more and more of this type and that God blesses them with more and more material blessings. Then we will be able to fund the kind of evangelism that will no doubt be required before our task is finished.

However, the spiritual challenges for both those with much money and those with little money are great. In 1 Timothy 6, Paul not only warns against the love of money—he provides the antidote for this sin. Verse 5 informs us that we cannot view godliness as a means of being blessed physically. The Israelites in the Old Testament days were often promised physical blessings for spiritual service, but the New Testament does not make the same connection. The examples of Jesus and the apostles should be sufficient to demonstrate this truth. God has promised to give us what we need, but not what we may want. In our materialistic society, we had better guard our hearts against the desire for more possessions, for they have a way of possessing us. Godliness is not the means to an end—riches—but the end itself, the goal of becoming holy even as our God is holy.

In 1 Timothy 6:6-7 Paul stresses the need for contentment with the basics of life. Are you content with food and clothing? This is what the text says. Let's just be honest about this one—who among us is really content with the basic essentials of life? Our list of necessities and luxuries is never static, for the latter category keeps seeping into the former. We are not easily satisfied materially, and we have a plethora of ways to rationalize it. Every time I start thinking about this subject, I am struck with the realization of how much I have and how little of it I would be eager to give up. We need to do a lot more examining of our hearts on this one, and we are going to have to include an inventory of our possessions in that examination. How much have we accumulated, why have we accumulated it, how are we using it, and how attached to it are we? Good questions, all. A truly sacrificial spirit is not easily found amidst plenteous possessions.

Contentment is a difficult state to achieve and maintain. It is not wrong to have possessions nor the success that produces them. The issue is much deeper. People wonder if advancement in their careers is counter to contentment. It often is, but it needn't be. Colossians 3:23-24 contains an all-important perspective on this subject, as it states:

> Whatever you do, work at it with all your heart, as working for the Lord, not for men, since you know that you will receive an inheritance from the Lord as a reward. It is the Lord Christ you are serving.

If we are seeking advancement, we may well be selfishly ambitious. If we are seeking to serve and glorify Christ in all that we do, our success will be a by-product of righteousness. Do you see the difference? One who is truly seeking God first in his life is content with little or much, for the physical things are very secondary to him. Paul put it this way in Philippians 4:12:

> I know what it is to be in need, and I know what it is to have plenty. I have learned the secret of being content in any and every situation, whether well fed or hungry, whether living in plenty or in want.

How content are you with what you have?

1 Timothy 6:9-12 instructs us to flee from the love of money, not simply by being afraid of it, but by developing righteous qualities and engaging in the good fight of the faith. We live in an age when people love things and use people, rather than loving people and using things. The difference between the two is huge. God, who has all things, loves only people. Why allow your life to be focused on what death will take away? What difference does it really make what kind of house you live in, or the car you drive or the clothes you wear? Be honest with your heart of hearts: how important are such things to you? The answer to these questions is not difficult to ascertain. Just take an inventory of your thought life and your schedule. You spend your time thinking about and doing what is most important to you.

> "No servant can serve two masters. Either he will hate the one and love the other, or he will be devoted to the one and despise the other. You cannot serve both God and Money." (Luke 16:13)

Who is master in your life? God knows and he wants you to know. Figure it out. Read James 2:1-4 and ask yourself how you view those who are rich materially, compared to those at the other end of the spectrum. Who we admire shows what we admire.

Finally, 1 Timothy 6:17-19 admonishes us to be rich in good deeds, which will include gracious generosity with our money. When we are blessed financially, it is for the purpose of giving to meet the physical and spiritual needs of others. The passage is addressed to the rich, and most of us in First World countries are just that in comparison with the rest of the world.

Worldly riches are very uncertain. While you have them, and to whatever extent you have them, use them to the glory of God. Focus on the spiritual side of life, and if God blesses you with more materially, enjoy it while it lasts and use it to the fullest extent to serve him and bless others.

We came into the world naked, and we will leave with nothing but a shroud. Clothe yourselves with righteousness, including a righteous view of money. Avoid the extremes of loving it or envying those who have more of it than you do. Whatever amount you have, use it well. In this way, your heart will remain spiritual.

> "Do not store up for yourselves treasures on earth, where moth and rust destroy, and where thieves break in and steal. But store up for yourselves treasures in heaven, where moth and rust do not destroy, and where thieves do not break in and steal. For where your treasure is, there your heart will be also." (Matthew 6:19-21)

To Help You Focus

1. Before reading this chapter, how would you define someone who is materialistic? Did your view change after reading it?

2. How content are you? Would your spouse or best friend agree with your answer? Ask him or her.

3. What is your favorite way of serving God and/or blessing others with your financial resources? Will you try to find another way also?

9
Escaping the Performance Trap

> But he said to me, "My grace is sufficient for
> you, for my power is made perfect in weak-
> ness." Therefore I will boast all the more gladly
> about my weaknesses, so that Christ's power
> may rest on me. That is why, for Christ's sake,
> I delight in weaknesses, in insults, in hardships,
> in persecutions, in difficulties. For when I am
> weak, then I am strong.
>
> 2 Corinthians 12:9-10

I have a book by Donald Seamands titled *Escaping the Performance Trap*. The book was first entitled *Healing Grace*, later changed to the performance motif, and recently changed back to the grace motif. Actually, both titles work well, for unless you really understand and appropriate God's grace, you cannot escape one of the least understood and most damaging tools of Satan.

Our world is steeped in the performance mentality, and probably most of us have been greatly affected by it. At the outset, it is important to note that performing well is not a negative thing. In fact, much about striving for excellence is, well, excellent! Who wants to fail when success can be enjoyed? Who does not want to improve as much as possible at any endeavor undertaken? As the old saying goes, "If it's worth doing, it's worth doing right." The performance trap we are describing has to do with what might be termed perfectionism. Those with perfectionist tendencies are not often satisfied. As a result, they often feel that they are not measuring up to their self-defined standards. And they normally inflict these anxieties onto others, especially family members.

Associated with the sense of failure is an accompanying sense of guilt. The term "neurotic guilt" is sometimes used in this connection, meaning that the guilt is not from a sin before God, but imagined guilt or self-inflicted guilt. Frankly, it is a malady that plagues a large percentage of the population—and not a few disciples. In the spiritual realm, we speak of those with "accused consciences," meaning that they often feel guilty about this failure to live up to their own idealistic standards of what they should have been and done. Religious people often struggle with these feelings, because it is not always easy to balance the Biblical call to do our best with the reality of our human frailty. Sin means literally "to miss the mark," and who of us does not miss the mark regularly and repeatedly? Surely we must learn to understand God's grace in order to be healed from our perfectionist tendencies and the ever-present sense of not measuring up. Guilt-ridden people are not joyful people, and frankly, they are poor advertisements for God's kingdom.

Where does this performance mentality come from? For many, it starts with noble intentions. We want to do our best, and certainly nobody can fault that. But when we begin to mix in pride, the road of life takes a wrong turn. We then enjoy the attention and praise that come from being outstanding, and achievement becomes a way to feel good about ourselves. Parental pride causes us to transfer this tendency to our children, and we want them to be high achievers—both for their sakes and for ours. The rub comes when excellence in *doing* takes precedence over excellence in *being*. Building character is far more important than amassing athletic records and topping out SAT scores. The children whose parents set unrealistic standards for them will begin packing and carrying around emotional baggage. If they are made to feel that no matter how well they do, they could have (should have) done even better, they are headed toward emotional damage and danger. The issue is subtle, however, because working hard is a part of building character. The problem is in how important performance becomes to us and the kinds of sacrifices we are willing to make for outstanding accomplishments.

Understanding our drive for success is paramount if we are to avoid emotional confusion, frustration and pain. One of the most helpful insights about the performance mode lies in understanding its connection with self-esteem. All of us develop insecurities in our lives—about our looks, our athletic or other abilities, our family backgrounds, or any one of a dozen things. Rejection, or fear of rejection, is at the root of most of our insecurities. The stronger the sense of rejection, the greater the insecurities. And to make matters worse, rejection comes in many forms, some obvious and some quite subtle.

So what do we do with these insecurities? Usually we go in one of two directions: we either pull back and risk little, hoping to avoid further failure with its sense of rejection, or we determine to prove ourselves through performance. Since we do not feel good about ourselves, we try to impress others into thinking well of us, believing that this will help us feel better. It is a vicious cycle in the end, and by midlife, we feel the crisis coming on. I decided years ago that midlife crises occur when we can no longer find the resolve to hold up our performance masks. We let them down and the real *us* comes out. Truthfully, much of our drive to succeed comes from this source of low self-esteem.

I remember reading in a popular magazine about a survey that was taken of high achieving businesspeople—the ones who always fly first class, are picked up in limousines and stay in five-star hotels. Their greatest fear was that people would discover that what they saw in these performers was not who they really were. In other words, they were playing the "I'm out to impress you" game, but deep inside knew that they were not nearly as impressive as the image they were striving mightily to portray. Sound familiar?

As a teen, some described me as having a superiority complex. The term is a misnomer, for no such complex exists. It is a cover-up for insecurities. It took me years to find the courage to peel away the mask and start being honest with who I was inside and how I felt about myself. In the interim, I looked for endeavors in which I could not only be successful, but be the best. Much of our competitiveness comes from this source. As much as I always loved sports, I was mediocre in them. I moved into the music realm, where I could be really outstanding. Of course, it is not wrong to migrate toward what we do best, but the reason for the migration may well be wrong. I my case it was prideful insecurities and a desire to prove myself. People who only talk about the successes in their lives are on this track, and the extent to which they avoid emotional vulnerability is a good measure of the extent of their insecurities.

The perfection-oriented performer tries to conceal insecurities by building a superimage of himself (or herself). He projects his strong points into this image, raised to their highest power, and eliminates his weaker points. He constantly emphasizes the strong points and resists all attempts of others to mention the weak ones. He may or may not seem defensive in dodging critiques, but dodge he will. He clings tenaciously to the projected image in an effort to earn respect from others and thereby feel good about himself. The fallacy of the whole system is that it is not really respect that we want. What we really want is love and acceptance. But we set ourselves up to block receiving what we need by trying to convince others that we are awesome. Now here is the kicker: Real love by Biblical definition is *unconditional*. To be loved, our negative points must be graciously accepted by others, not just our positive points. Therefore, unless we are open about our negative points, we will never really feel loved! This is a hugely important point, without which we cannot progress as human beings and certainly not as disciples of Jesus Christ. No wonder Paul was so open about his sins and weaknesses. (Read again very carefully his words from 2 Corinthians 12:9-10 at the beginning of this chapter.)

Paul as a Pharisee was a performer par excellence (Philippians 3:4-6). He was as works oriented as anyone could be. His drive for success made him perhaps the top student of Gamaliel, the most revered rabbi in Israel (Acts 22:3). These guys were good. Their standard for life was very, very high. They lived up to it in remarkable ways, but they trusted in their performance as the basis of a right standing with God. Such a mentality prompted writings like Romans and Galatians. No excellence of spiritual performance is going to earn a relationship with God. He knows all of our sins, including heart sins and hidden sins. God cannot be duped by our superimages, and to cut to the chase, not many others are for very long. We can play the ostrich, sticking our heads into the sand and denying the bad stuff in us, but all the while, others are observing everything else sticking out! It is time to get real with ourselves and others.

Paul the Christian was not looking for love in all the wrong places (in performance). He opened up his life and heart and invited others in. Look at what he wrote in 2 Corinthians 6:11-13:

> We have spoken freely to you, Corinthians, and
> opened wide our hearts to you. We are not with-
> holding our affection from you, but you are with-
> holding yours from us. As a fair exchange—I speak
> as to my children—open wide your hearts also.
> (2 Corinthians 6:11-13)

God's ways are usually about 180 degrees opposite from man's ways. The worldly approach is to tell all of the positive stuff about ourselves and to keep the negative hidden. After we brag on ourselves in this way, we have only a gnawing, hollow feeling left. God says to keep all of the good stuff to ourselves and to tell all of the negative. At the end of this process, we are left with a warm and fuzzy feeling, knowing that God sees the good and will reward us for it, while people will see the bad and extend unconditional love to us. What could be better?

Learning to pull back the curtain on my heart was an arduous and often painful process. I would be open about my negative things and later be struck with the panicky feeling of, "What have I done?" Through the years, I discovered one of the kingdom's greatest secrets: The more I tell people what a wretch I am, the more they think I am awesome. It is an amazing phenomenon, but it has this effect every time. People realize the difficulty of real transparency, and when you open wide your hearts to them, they are drawn to you like a magnet.

I appreciate the encouragement I receive from people regarding my speaking or writing gifts, and I am grateful to

God for the gifts and the opportunities to use them. Recognition and respect are good, as long as we realize that all good things come from God and not from us. But what I appreciate most are simply open and sincere expressions of love, not for what I have done, but for who I want to be for God and for others.

I will not say that I have escaped totally from the performance trap, for it has steel jaws at times, but I will say that I understand it intellectually. Further, I will also say that I am happiest when I emotionally grasp the truth of the gospel and relax enough to accept the love from God and others that I so much need. Won't you join me?

To Help You Focus

1. What elements in your background may have caused you to be vulnerable to the performance trap?

2. Why does the message of the gospel make such a difference in helping us escape from that trap? Do you relentlessly apply the gospel's message to your mind and heart?

3. How does getting open about your sin and your weaknesses help set you free?

10
Don't Cry over Spilt Milk!

> Not that I have already obtained all this, or
> have already been made perfect, but I press on
> to take hold of that for which Christ Jesus took
> hold of me. Brothers, I do not consider myself
> yet to have taken hold of it. But one thing I do:
> Forgetting what is behind and straining to-
> ward what is ahead, I press on toward the goal
> to win the prize for which God has called me
> heavenward in Christ Jesus.
>
> Philippians 3:12-14

Most of us heard at a fairly early age, "Don't cry over spilt milk." Funny thing, though—my father often made me cry over spilt milk (or spilt soda, or spilt coffee or spilt iced tea). Somehow the spills hooked his emotions, and he became upset at the *spiller*, even when he himself was the guilty party. Of course, the saying means that after making a mistake, we should not languish in it. We must put it behind us and move on in positive directions. It is a good admonition for everyone, but there is a spiritual way to do this that I believe only disciples can grasp.

To handle mistakes spiritually does not mean denying them and "stuffing" them deep inside. This causes them to putrefy and corrode our hearts and keeps us from becoming better people and better people helpers. But what about you? Do you cry over spilt milk? Are you solution oriented, or do you stay locked in the "what if" or "if only" mode? Much of our challenge is in accepting failures without feeling like failures. One way to meet this challenge is to become what we might call "process thinkers," rather than terminal thinkers. Process thinkers see any specific situation as only a part of the picture, but terminal thinkers tend to see it as the whole picture. Stated another way, the former views life as through a video camera (an ongoing process, with the opportunity to overcome mistakes), whereas the latter views it as a snapshot (you are "captured" in your mistakes of the moment).

A few years back, Theresa and I were asked to help a young Christian couple. They were having more than a normal share of marital difficulties. We met with them both as a couple the first time, but quickly realized that most of their marriage problems were attitudinal, tracing back to perspectives produced in them by their families long before they married each other. Someone has said that six people are intricately involved in any marriage: the couple and each of their parents. The acorn does not fall far from the tree, for children develop their parents' views of life almost from birth. In this counseling situation, we spent time with the two mates separately as we helped them to untangle their unspiritual thinking. (Of course, I spent my time helping the husband.) Our conversations centered around the effects of a performance mind-set—the way we view ourselves and others, especially in view of failures and weaknesses. The husband tended to see his failures as utterly calamitous, and weaknesses in those with whom he had close relationships (particularly his parents) as very difficult to accept. He was a terminal thinker, not a process thinker.

Peter and Judas were both betrayers. Judas was the consummate example of a terminal thinker, whereas Peter was less so. Actually, Peter also seemed to give up hope, but he did not kill himself, which allowed Jesus to reach out and restore him. My thought is that if Judas had not killed himself, Jesus would have in fact reached out to him after the resurrection. God is never a terminal thinker in the way he views humans, and only death removes opportunity.

If we view mistakes as a part of a growth process, then we are not blown away by our failures or the failures of others. We must mature in seeing the failures and weaknesses of significant others in our lives, especially parents, without feeling negative or resentful toward them. If they are non-Christians, then we can expect them to act like non-Christians. In areas in which we are the guilty ones, we must learn to accept responsibility in a mature, spiritual way without going to the extremes of denying reality or flagellating ourselves.

If we are of a performance mind-set, then we become upset enough about our failures to try to minimize them, or we become despondent over them. We tend to blame

God, others or ourselves. With this distorted concept, we may shoulder the blame at times to protect those who are also guilty, perhaps more guilty than we, when we should not. Those who were abused by family members sometimes are critical of themselves, rather than seeing where the blame really belongs.

Terminal thinkers become decimated by failure and try to avoid calling it that, but process thinkers face the facts, repent quickly and move on, having learned from the experience. We must learn from our mistakes, repent of the sins we committed, formulate a plan to do better in the future, and start over with a cleansed conscience. God is the God of new beginnings, but only if we accept that the gospel allows us to start over again and again.

In one sense, the key to the future is the past. If we process our failures and those of others in the proper way, we can deal with whatever happened. In many cases, we can even smile at the failures of the past as we embrace the lessons learned from them. Of course, if the consequences of our sins affected others significantly, it will never be a lighthearted matter. For example, Peter probably reached the point of at least not being smitten in conscience when the daily alarm-clock rooster crowed. In Paul's case, his persecution involved very serious consequences in the families of those who were killed, and those memories surely always brought pain. But he was sobered and motivated by them, rather than carrying his guilt and being demotivated and crippled emotionally.

Failure to achieve our dreams constitutes one of our greatest challenges from our pasts. We set our hearts on doing or achieving something spiritually, and when these dreams die, they die hard. Many disciples deal with the failure of overt sin better than they deal with the failure to achieve "kingdom dreams." Death of any type, including the death of dreams, always is followed by a time of mourning and grief. The symptoms are much the same, regardless of the type of death being grieved over. Shock and denial, the first stage, gives way to anger and then to depression or apathy. But, if processed righteously, acceptance of the death is reached, and we feel resolved and at peace once again.

However, those who do not understand that the death of dreams requires a grief process are often unequipped to work through it. They maintain a sense of failure and can think that God has rejected them. They either become angry and resentful or find most of their spiritual motivation swallowed up by apathy. In this case, the "spilt milk" they cry over is a failure to reach their self-defined spiritual goals and dreams. Thoughts of what might have been flood their souls, and the present is rendered mediocre (or worse) by this contemplation of the past. What can you do in this case? Simply stated, don't give in to terminal thinking. Realize that what has happened is all a part of the process God is taking you through to bring you to his higher purposes.

God always has a plan to prosper us and to bless our futures. He is that kind of Father and will never be otherwise. Our tendency to see spirituality as based on performance and achievement blocks our vision and allows Satan to hurt us deeply. What really matters in life anyway? How about being right with God, enjoying a growing relationship with him, helping others get right with God and helping them enjoy a growing relationship with him—aren't these the big issues? If we do these things, whether we are leaders or not, on the ministry staff or not, on a mission team or not, we will be fulfilled and happy. The performance mind-set many in the kingdom still have, and the accompanying tendency to be terminal thinkers rather than process thinkers, is more destructive than we realize. Why not rather just focus on enjoying God and helping others to enjoy him?

A million years from now, when we are rejoicing in heaven, what difference will it make whether we were evangelists or garden-variety disciples? Let's learn to accept ourselves, warts and all, and to come to peace with the less-than-ideal in our pasts. God has promised that all of it will be used by him to work out good ends for us (Romans 8:28). Why fret and worry? Life is too short and eternity too long to allow an unspiritual view of life's disappointments to rob us of our joy in Jesus and to cripple us emotionally and spiritually. Because of the gospel, we have good reason to just do what the little song says, "Don't worry, be happy." I think that God will be happy, too!

To Help You Focus

1. How have you allowed disappointments in life or the failure to achieve "kingdom dreams" to rob you of your joy?

2. When faced with failure, what helps you to learn from the experience and move on?

3. Do you become shocked and resentful because of the failures of significant others in your life, such as your parents or your spouse? What can you change in order to be able to view these in a mature and spiritual way?

4. Do you trust God's promises to prosper you, to bless you and to work all things together for your good? What scriptures could you memorize to help you to remember God's promises?

The Power of Negative Thinking

> But the men who had gone up with him said, "We can't attack those people; they are stronger than we are." And they spread among the Israelites a bad report about the land they had explored. They said, "The land we explored devours those living in it. All the people we saw there are of great size. We saw the Nephilim there (the descendants of Anak come from the Nephilim). We seemed like grasshoppers in our own eyes, and we looked the same to them."
>
> Numbers 13:31-33

If there is power in positive thinking (especially *spiritual* positive thinking!), there is also power in the opposite. Of course, this power is satanic in nature, and using it will accomplish his ends rather than God's. But without question, we are trained by our families and by our cultures to be negative in our evaluations of ourselves, others and circumstances. The most cursory glance at any newspaper will provide plenty of proof for this. Years ago, I vividly remember hearing a radio report of a study that was conducted to evaluate the results of those who characteristically thought negatively and those who thought positively. The findings of the study indicated that the negative thinkers were much more accurate in their assessments of situations, but the positive thinkers were able to produce positive results out of negative situations. Even those without a true spiritual perspective have figured out that negative thinking produces negative results.

One of the most graphic Biblical accounts showing the power of negative thinking is Numbers 13, the record of the twelve spies sent to spy out Canaan. In reading this account, several obvious lessons show us paths to avoid at all costs. One lesson is that the negative often excites stronger emotions than does the positive. In spite of the faith-filled pleas of Joshua and Caleb, the two spies with a good report, the nation was easily and strongly swayed by the negative report. They quickly forgot God's amazing miracles and victories and were absolutely filled with "grasshopper thinking."

As humans, we are so prone to assume the worst and believe the worst. We focus on what is wrong or on what we are afraid will go wrong. Negative thinking is a pervasive tendency. It must be seen as what it is—an unloving, unfaithful response to God's promises. In terms of Paul's definition of love in 1 Corinthians 13, spiritual thinking which is loving means that we do not delight in evil but rejoice with the truth—always protecting, always trusting, always hoping, always persevering (vv6-7).

A second lesson gleaned from Numbers 13 is that a majority of people inevitably practice negative thinking. In this case, the ratio was ten to two among the spies and presumably a million to one in the multitude. We would much rather curse the darkness than light a candle. Those who do not jump to negative conclusions and think the worst are thought to be strange. No wonder so many people reacted negatively to Jesus. He was completely realistic about man's sinful condition, but he was full of faith and confident that men could be changed by God's power. The leaders of his time thought that he was demon-possessed. The narrow road of Matthew 7:13-14 is the path of a small minority. Only eight people in Noah's day were able to rise above the crowd and trust in the promises of God (1 Peter 3:20). In Elijah's day, thankfully there were 7,000 who had refused to bow the knee to Baal (1 Kings 19:18), but that was a small minority in Israel. In the aftermath of the crucifixion, how many were confident that resurrection would follow? Next to nil. If we are to follow Jesus, we had better get comfortable with always being in a minority and with being thought of as weird by the majority. I've got to love the church—it's the only place where I am really accepted as somewhat normal!

A third lesson from Numbers 13 is that negativism is deceptive to observers. It seems so, well, *normal*. Since Satan is the great deceiver, this should not come as any surprise. What does come as a surprise is how completely we can all be deceived by sin at times. We can feel that we are doing right with a perfectly clear conscience, only to discover later that we were wrong in a matter. The problem is that the negative view has quite a lot of reality to commend it, and it's often mixed with some positives.

For example, in Numbers 13:27-28, we read this report of the spies:

> They gave Moses this account: "We went into the land to which you sent us, and it does flow with milk and honey! Here is its fruit. But the people who live there are powerful, and the cities are fortified and very large. We even saw descendants of Anak there."
> (Numbers 13:27-28)

Although the negative was prefaced with the positive, the negative carried the day. In our conversation, the content following the conjunction "but" shows convincingly whether we are focused on the positives or not. If we end with the negative, it will lodge in our hearts and the hearts of others. Being realistic with the facts is good, but ending with faith is better—it's essential. Note the difference in the two reports given to the Israelites:

> Then Caleb silenced the people before Moses and said, "We should go up and take possession of the land, for we can certainly do it."
> But the men who had gone up with him said, "We can't attack those people; they are stronger than we are." (Numbers 13:30-31)

How are you at being focused on the positives about situations and other people? Do you justify negativity by claiming that you must deal honestly with reality? In Romans 4:19, we find that Abraham faced the facts of his situation, but then he "faithed" them. The facts are the facts are the facts, but God is greater than any reality that blocks what he wants done in our lives. It is not, "God is powerful and good, but look at these worrisome facts." It must rather be, "the worrisome facts are present, but God is bigger and stronger than any combination of them."[1]

Faith looks beyond humanistic realities to divine possibilities. The physical components and characteristic of water are such that man cannot walk on it, but try convincing Peter of that one! (Matthew 14:28-29). God is God, and we cannot be deceived into allowing our faith to be destroyed in any situation, however challenging it may seem from a human viewpoint.

A fourth lesson from Kadesh Barnea (where the spies were sent out from) should be quite obvious: Leaders have the most responsibility for determining the thinking of the group they lead. However, the followers who are influenced by them are absolutely responsible for their choices. The whole nation was punished for their lack of faith, not just the leaders. What a tragedy! Just think of what might have been. After leaving Egypt, the Israelites could have gone quickly into the promised land. Forty years of attending funerals could have been averted (all of those twenty years old or older had to die before the nation could enter Canaan). Negative thinking shows up first in leadership. Only if leaders are positive do you find out who the negative thinkers are back in the pack (and some are always there).

Leaders have the God-given responsibility to lead, but followers have the responsibility to follow. Hebrews 13:17 says:

[1] A more complete examination of this can be found in *Mind Change: The Overcomer's Handbook* by Thomas A. Jones (Woburn, Mass: Discipleship Publications International, 1996).

Obey your leaders and submit to their authority. They keep watch over you as men who must give an account. Obey them so that their work will be a joy, not a burden, for that would be of no advantage to you. (Hebrews 13:17)

The Greek term translated "submit to their authority" means literally to "be persuaded." True, leaders must be willing to reason and persuade, but the passage is addressed to followers. They must have a will to be persuaded, to be open to changing their minds.

As a leader who often deals with various problem situations, I encounter negative thinkers who are very difficult to convince. They lock onto something in the church that they don't like and seem to relish holding on to the negative thinking that makes them miserable. I often compare them to people studying the Bible who cannot seem to see past their preconceived views of the requirements for being saved. Unless they really determine to open their hearts to new truths, perhaps by prayer and fasting, they simply cannot and will not see it. Those locked in negative thinking are in the same boat. Unless they change their will to believe, they will remain locked in their negativity and may ultimately lose their salvation.

A fifth and final lesson from the spying out of Canaan is that negativism is tragic in its results. It destroys the faith of individuals and the unity of groups that God would otherwise be able to bless. In the case of these Israelites, a change of mind did not alleviate the consequences. Read

Numbers 14:36-45. The passage is a chilling reminder of the tragedy that follows unfaithful thinking and acting. God is always willing to forgive our guilt, but some consequences cannot be undone. How many times have we wished that we could turn back the clock and start over? But alas, it cannot be done. We must see the power of negativity and avoid it like the plague it is. When you begin to lack faith about anything, rest assured that Satan is near. True, we need to recognize when something is wrong, but then we must look for godly solutions. Entertaining negative thoughts with no plan to change the situation is dangerous to our spiritual health.

The power of spiritual thinking lies in part with our consistent refusal to think negatively. Let us be convinced that thinking this way is not like Jesus. Let's learn these lessons well and avoid being used by Satan. At one time, these men were revered leaders in Israel: Shammua, Shaphat, Igal, Palti, Gaddiel, Gaddi, Ammiel, Sethur, Nahbi and Geuel. Now no one even remembers the names of these ten unfaithful spies. But we all know Joshua and Caleb, and their names inspire us to this day. Let us live with faith as they did. Let us confront the most difficult and challenging circumstances and say, "God is still at work and he still has a plan." The power of negative thinking or the power of spiritual thinking—the choice is yours!

To Help You Focus

1. How can one be a positive thinker but not necessarily a positive *spiritual* thinker? Why is it important to understand the difference?

2. Would those closest to you say that you approach challenges with faith or with negative thinking?

3. What spiritual discipline is needed in your life to keep your thinking spiritually positive?

I Was Born This Way!

> You shall not bow down to them or worship them; for I, the Lord your God, am a jealous God, punishing the children for the sin of the fathers to the third and fourth generation of those who hate me.
>
> Deuteronomy 5:9

> The soul who sins is the one who will die. The son will not share the guilt of the father, nor will the father share the guilt of the son. The righteousness of the righteous man will be credited to him, and the wickedness of the wicked will be charged against him.
>
> Ezekiel 18:20

Are we a product of environment or heredity? This question has been raised in the mind of virtually every human being and debated hotly by a fair number of them (including me). As a young man, I was almost totally on the side of environment. I agreed with philosopher John Locke who postulated that we are born with a tabula rasa, a blank slate, on which life's experiences indelibly imprint our future tendencies and directions. Then I met people who had been adopted at birth and who later were reunited with their birth parents. They were uncannily similar to their birth parents. (Even in the kingdom of God, I can think of at least one striking example of such.) Also, I see in people some propensities in certain directions that cannot be explained without the influence of their gene pool. I concluded that the answer to the environment or heredity question is simply *yes*, both/and—rather than either/or.

Having said this, we must be very careful how we view this issue. Some of us go to the extreme of discounting heredity almost entirely in the areas of emotional make-up and physical constitution. In our phobia of psychology, we make those who are struggling with things that they do not really understand about themselves feel untrusted. But God is the author of all laws of the universe, whether it be the law of gravity or the law of the psyche, and understanding the truths within any of them can be very beneficial on a practical level.

I have found that our emotions, intellect and body are all very connected, and anything that affects us in one of those areas affects us in others. Therefore, those who do have ill-defined physical challenges usually have emotional and spiritual challenges as well. Who of us feels as positive and faithful when we are sick as we do when we are healthy? If we are afraid that others with physical or emotional challenges are going to use them as excuses, we will develop suspicions that are perceived at an emotional level by those with the problems—even if we do not express our concerns verbally. We must be slow to judge in situations that we do not understand completely. If we are unsympathetic and cynical toward those with certain problems, God may one day bless us with an understanding gained by our own enrollment in the school of hard knocks—perhaps with the very same problem.

The other extreme encountered in viewing how we became who we are is when we develop a victim mentality regarding ourselves or others. Hence, the title of this chapter is "I was born this way." Need it even be said that our modern world is steeped in this doctrine? We are told that our propensity to be angry, use drugs, be immoral or just about anything else is likely due to some inherited gene. What an un-Biblical, revolting doctrine! Who can believe it?! Most feel that we are either born a certain way or shaped a certain way with irrevocable results. However, those who supposedly hold to such theories will have extreme difficulty harmonizing them with the case of someone killing or maiming their own child. We quickly abandon theory when the rigid rod of reality hits close to home. But we are nonetheless predisposed to think in terms of a victim mentality until such reality does invade our space.

I remember years ago counseling a person with an abused background who had quite a challenge with submission to anyone, including God. For some time, I excused the person's lack of trust, keeping in mind the terror of their early life experiences. No wonder they found it very difficult to trust any authority—they had been abused by an authority figure! Eventually it dawned on me that dozens of other disciples with the same background had learned to trust again and had developed a very spiritual understanding of submission. Why was there a difference? The answer is very simple: One type had decided to repent of his or her mistrust, no matter how great the challenge of doing so, and the other had not. It boiled down to a matter of heart. Certain Biblical injunctions are more difficult for us as individuals than are others, due to our backgrounds, but the commands are not thereby eliminated or lessened. God still expects us to do what he says, which means that by his power we can do it. He does not ask us to do anything he will not enable us to do.

I also recall talking at length to disciples who seemed stuck in their problems and sins. Talking through their pasts was a part of developing an understanding of how they became as they were. In learning about the struggles they had been through, I sometimes found myself being not only sympathetic, but also sentimental (which never helps anyone). Finally, I came to my senses and quit complicating the situation with too much of a psychological approach. I had to remember that no matter what the emotional and psychological damage, their ultimate problem had now become sin. I just needed to look for the specific sins involved, call them by Biblical names and help the person see that God called for repentance. When this happens, everyone breathes a sigh of relief (including the one in sin—maybe *especially* the one in sin) because a solution is in view. The solution is always to identify the sin, repent of it, start relying on God's grace and formulate a plan to overcome the sin.

I will always defend the need for using some psychological principles in helping understand how people developed their problems, since Satan uses these problems to sow his sins deep in the heart. On the other hand, psychology is only useful for determining the root causes of problems. *It is powerless in providing the solution—only God can do that.* A doctor may examine and determine the nature of an illness, but having a diagnosis does not solve the problem. It takes an effective treatment to cure the disease. The same is true spiritually. We can dig into a person's background to understand them and their problems better, but only Biblical principles wrought by the Holy Spirit can bring about God's cure. I find myself concerned about both those who eschew psychology and those who trust it too much. We must use any principle that helps, because all true principles in any realm come ultimately from God, but our trust can never be in the principle or the technique itself. As James put it, "Every good and perfect gift is from above, coming down from the Father of the heavenly lights" (James 1:17).

Most importantly, we must see that God can help us overcome our sinful tendencies, whether they trace back to inheritance or environment. Some people get absolutely paranoid about their family history. They have a sense of angst about their futures. For example, perhaps mental illness was present in several ancestors. While it is possible that tendencies in this direction due to chemical imbalance may be inherited, for the most part, anyone with enough faith in God can break the cycle. The healing process, in more severe cases, may have to involve the work of mental health professionals, but it is the faith of the individual in combination with this work that brings true change.

I have met multitudes of disciples whose families were filled with all kinds of emotional disturbances, and yet they were radically different. They accepted the promises of God and did not allow themselves to become self-fulfilling prophets and prophetesses through anxieties and phobias. By faith, they broke the cycle. In my emotional makeup, I am most like the side of my family that is characterized by emotional imbalance. Yet, I have depended on God to break the cycle in me, and he has. God has broken the cycle for large numbers of people and I am persuaded that he can do it for all of us, if we will reject the thinking that allows Satan to keep the cycle going.

One of the greatest examples in the Old Testament to show that we are not bound by our families or circumstances is that of the kings of Judah. Hezekiah was one of the few good kings in the lineage of David, but both his father and grandfather were evil before him. However, he broke the cycle. Then, both his son Manasseh and his grandson Amon were very wicked. Next came Josiah, perhaps the greatest king in the history of the divided kingdom. In spite of their gene pools and the terrible examples of their families, both Hezekiah and Josiah rose above what life had dealt to them. They made righteous choices and were able to change the destiny to which they fell heir.

The promises of God are far greater than our past and present challenges. Let's decide to believe them and refuse to be victims of Satan. If God be God, the victory is ours for the taking.

> And we pray this in order that you may live a life worthy of the Lord and may please him in every way: bearing fruit in every good work, growing in the knowledge of God, being strengthened with all power according to his glorious might so that you may have great endurance and patience, and joyfully giving thanks to the Father, who has qualified you to share in the inheritance of the saints in the kingdom of light. (Colossians 1:10-12)

To Help You Focus

1. In what ways are you tempted to blame either your heredity or your upbringing for your behavior?

2. While it is not helpful to excuse our behavior ever, why is it helpful to understand our roots?

3. What promises of God need to be applied to the issues you thought about in the first question?

13

Disappointed

> "O Jerusalem, Jerusalem, you who kill the prophets and stone those sent to you, how often I have longed to gather your children together, as a hen gathers her chicks under her wings, but you were not willing."
>
> Matthew 23:37

"I am so disappointed in you." Have you ever been on the receiving end of statements like this one? Surely all of us would say yes, and surely we would all agree that it's difficult to hear such statements without getting our feelings hurt. I hate to be disappointed, and I dread even more the thought of disappointing others. What a sinking feeling—to be a disappointment to those whom I love most!

I believe that we really don't understand the lack of spirituality that lies behind our frequent disappointments in others. Hopefully, in this chapter we will tread new ground for most readers, resulting in a better view of others, of ourselves and of life generally. Disappointed people are not happy people. By God's grace, we can decrease the disappointment level in our lives substantially—and this cannot accomplish anything but good.

The dictionary defines "disappointed" in this way: "depressed or discouraged by the failure of one's hopes or expectations." Immediately we see that most words in this definition (depressed, discouraged, failure) are negative in tone and certainly not desirable in the hearts of Jesus' followers.

What does the Bible say about this subject? Actually, the Bible does not use the word "disappoint" (in its various forms) in the same sense as we do. Biblically, its meaning is more along the lines of being ashamed. Being ashamed is primarily a result of our own sin and not simply a feeling—and certainly not a feeling directed at others. One thing is clear: Some ideas that are common to us, including the idea of God being disappointed in us, are not spoken of in the Bible.

Disappointment in others exposes a basic selfishness in the one feeling disappointed. Stated another way, when you see someone not living up to his or her potential, you feel either primarily concerned for the person or else hurt (disappointed) for yourself. Think about that for a moment. If this is true, God feels *concern* for us when we fail, not disappointment, since disappointment by definition is rather self-focused. Think about people you would describe as real servants, real givers. Are they prone to disappointment in others? Or are they not much more likely to feel concern for those who may not have made the best choices, even if those choices have an effect on them?

I can picture many parents being in a position similar to that of the father (God) in the Parable of the Lost Son in

Luke 15. However, unlike God, they would be very quick to say, "I told you so." Or, they would share in vivid detail how the sinful child has hurt them deeply and the anguish of heart and sleepless nights they endured as a result. However, in the Gospel account, the father was extremely quick to forgive and move on, without any reference to the personal pain endured as a result of the son's pigpen behavior. We would very likely be filled with disappointment, but God was filled only with compassion for the sinner. Thank God that he is not like us!

Most of us assume that God often views us with a disappointed heart, but not because the Bible ever says it. We assume it because our very human parents typically expressed disappointment in us with painful regularity, showing their own self-focus. God has no selfishness in him at all and thus is not characterized by disappointment. Is that not a comfort to you?

Look back at the verse at the beginning of the chapter. At first glance, it would seem that Jesus was expressing disappointment in the people of Jerusalem. Certainly he was feeling pain, but was it pain for himself—the pain of rejection—or was it pain for lost souls? A parallel passage clears this one up for us.

> As he approached Jerusalem and saw the city, he wept over it and said, "If you, even you, had only known on this day what would bring you peace—but now it is hidden from your eyes." (Luke 19:41-42)

I don't know how all of this strikes you, but it leaves me with a great sense of relief. I understand God's love better. Our inclination is to think that God is disappointed in us when we sin and turns away until we repent (or have time to suffer, to do penance!), at which time he turns back to us in love once more. This may have been the way our parents reacted to our undesirable behavior, but it is not even close to how God reacts to our sins. He is filled with concern for us and is totally solution oriented. (Of course, God does become angry with those who are habitually locked into deliberate sins. But that is not the heart of a disciple; we sin, but this is neither our heart nor our habit.) As a father, my concern is heightened when my children are struggling with something, and at that time, they get more genuine attention than when they are doing well. My feelings are much more prone to be those of concern, rather than those of disappointment.

How about you? Are you often disappointed in yourself or in others? If so, examine your heart in this matter. Recently, I have been thinking about the underlying qualities that result in humility, for humility is surely one of the attitudes that God treasures and blesses most. He resists the proud and gives grace to the humble (1 Peter 5:5). But how does humility show up in our daily lives? In a myriad of ways, perhaps, but selflessness is surely one of the greatest ways. Selfishness and pride are probably the two most serious blights in our hearts and on our souls. Denying self is the first requirement of following Jesus. Selflessness is a prime characteristic of deity, and we are called to be imitators of God. Those who are self-absorbed and self-focused are selfish people (surprise, surprise!). Being selfish, they are not humble. They take things personally and selfishly and are often disappointed in others.

As a leader, I work with many other leaders. Through the years, I have observed certain tendencies. Some react quickly and become upset when they find that another leader has something against them; some have the opposite reaction of wanting to get together with those who are critical of them in order to resolve the issue. Leaders or not, we generally fit into one of these two camps. Which one do you fall into? One is self-absorbed and the second is others-absorbed. God is obviously in the latter category. Disappointed often? Selfish often! Frustrated at others often? Selfish often! Angry when others have things against you? Selfish once more!

The answer to our disappointments in and frustration with other people is found in Philippians 2:3-4.

> Do nothing from selfish ambition or conceit, but in humility regard others as better than yourselves. Let each of you look not to your own interests, but to the interests of others. (NRSV)

This is quoted from the New Revised Standard Version, because verse 4 is more literally rendered. Look not to your own interests, but to those of others. Obviously, we are going to look at our own interests to some degree, as the New International Version translation indicates, but Paul is using a part of speech here, called hyperbole, which makes an overstatement for the purpose of emphasis.

If we are humble enough to consider others better than ourselves, we will be focused on their feelings more than on our own feelings. If we are much more interested in looking at the interests of others than at our own, then we will feel much more concern and much less disappointment. A lack of spirituality shows up in pride, self-focus and subsequent disappointments. Conversely, spirituality is characterized by humility; humility is characterized by selflessness; and selflessness is characterized by a genuine concern for others.

Disappointment is the un-Godlike quality of selfishness. Concern is the godly quality, which comes from self-denial and *agape* love.

To Help You Focus

1. Is it easy for other people to disappoint you? What might this be showing you about you?

2. What are some of the things in others that cause you to be disappointed in them? How does this chapter give you a new way of looking at these things?

3. The next time you find yourself thinking "I am so disappointed in...," what would be a much more spiritual way to think?

The Big Black Brothers' Club

> You are all sons of God through faith in Christ
> Jesus, for all of you who were baptized into
> Christ have clothed yourselves with Christ. There
> is neither Jew nor Greek, slave nor free, male
> nor female, for you are all one in Christ Jesus.
> Galatians 3:26-28

Spiritual thinking, in one sense, means that we are colorblind, but it means more than that. In another sense, it means that we are both color-aware and color-appreciative. The Galatians passage above affirms that in some sense, physical distinctions are ended in Christ. Regardless of race, social status or gender, we are all equally valuable to our Creator. None is superior and none is inferior, for we are all made in the image of God and saved by the blood of Jesus. But we do not cease to be who we are racially, socially and sexually. Men are still men and women are still women. We must remain aware of those differences if we are to be effective evangelistically. (Paul was certainly thinking about this when he made his comments in 1 Corinthians 9:19-23 about becoming all things to all men to reach as many as possible.)

We must also be appreciative of the differences that remain. America is a blending of cultures like few other countries. Of course, in our cosmopolitan world, the cultural and racial composition of most nations is far more varied than in the past. However, Americans generally relish the variations more than the norm, since we were built with this diversity from the beginning. We are the big melting pot, and the acceptance of this diversity is at least a part of the reason many from other countries would like to migrate here. Financial opportunity is the biggest draw, made more attractive because these opportunities are found in a setting where backgrounds do not mean as much.

However, in spite of this relatively accepting atmosphere, prejudices abound. I was raised at a time and in a part of America where blacks and whites were quite segregated. I did not attend school with blacks until postgraduate studies, when I trained as a minister. (Thankfully, that all seems so strange now.) When I was a teen, I did construction work in the summers as "a common laborer," and most in that category were black workers. Being around black men on the job was the first time I was able to closely associate with them on a peer basis, and frankly, both they and I loved it. We had a blast acting more than a little crazy together. I enjoyed their fun-loving ways to no end, and my life was enriched by close association with those who were different from me racially and culturally. Some of my closest friends have been from different minorities ever since I was a young adult. As I learned from their cultures and backgrounds, I grew to delight in our differences.

The church in the Bible consisted of equals, but equals with some significant differences. Learning to love each other and live together as one body was not always easy, but it was and will always be God's way. Churches whose membership consists of all one race stand in stark contrast to the early church that Jesus built. Variety is the spice of life. We need each other, and we need to be enriched by the differences in each other. I rejoice in the true kingdom of God because it is such a conglomeration of different types of people. We have the rich and the poor; the educated and the uneducated; the young and the old; the socially adept and the socially inept; the blacks, the whites, the Asians and the Hispanics, and then mixtures of all of these. We are the same in heart and purpose, but not the same in so many other ways, and these differences are cause to rejoice. Only God could bring such a group together in love and harmony. Our unity is the demonstration to the world that we are true disciples of Jesus (John 13:34-35, 17:20-23).

On my desk is a very unusual picture of seven men, affectionately called the BBB Club—the Big Black Brothers' Club. A number of years ago, several brothers in the church started coming over to our house to watch Monday Night Football on television. Most of these brothers were black, and gradually, the moniker of "the BBBs" came into use. So, by mutual agreement, I am also black on Monday nights. (Actually, I always thought that I had too much soul to be a white man anyway!) Sometimes we discuss whether to invite a "token white" for the evening (remember, I'm black on Mondays). It is quite a group. Although a number of different "brother-brothers" (black disciples) have attended at different times, our club ended up with seven members: Bob Peterson, Walter Parrish, Curt Garner, Keith Avery, Jon Williams, Arthur Conard and me. My wife says that she can hear us out in the street, even though we meet in the basement. Playing spades and gin rummy often competes with the football game, and to say that it is a lively meeting is to downplay the true nature of the atmosphere considerably.

These brothers seem to understand that I need a setting where I am not expected to be an elder, but only one of the brothers, to be able to let my hair (what I have left) down completely. I need these men. I cherish our times together. Now that others have heard about us, they clamor to get into the fray. With good-natured but raucous humor, we give them a hard time and let them know that according to our bylaws, visitors must be approved by a majority of the club members. None of those little, white, skinny guys have much of a chance of approval! (Actually, those who do come have a great chance of losing their skinniness, since the food items are not exactly of the low-fat variety.)

The picture to which I referred earlier is very unusual because it was taken after Arthur died suddenly of heart arrest last fall at age thirty-eight. With the help of a friend, Arthur's picture was scanned into a computer along with our picture (taken later), and now we have the seven originals in a BBB Club picture. He had a heart condition and realized that he would not live a normal life span, yet he was as full of zest for life as anyone I have ever known. Deeply in love with God and people, he spent his last hours out sharing his faith. Returning home on the bus, he simply went to sleep and woke up with God.

Approximately seven hundred people from all walks of life attended his memorial service. The BBBs, along with several of Arthur's closest brothers, wept together at his casket. But during the day, we laughed about as often as we cried. Our tears were not for him, but for ourselves. He will be missed greatly by his faithful wife, Joyce, and by a vast throng of friends and family who loved him deeply. Life for us will not be the same, both because he leaves a void and because he changed us by his copious love and laughter. My background was about as different from Arthur's as one could imagine, but we were (are) brothers, and on Monday nights, brother-brothers.

In our racially tense society, people are more than impressed at our camaraderie and deeply appreciated love for one another. Where else can you find such relationships outside the family of God? We are in no way uptight about our differences; we glory in them. God made us as we are, and he expects us to enjoy each other to the full.

Any family in which all the children were exactly alike would be boring at best. The diversity of nature demonstrates God's belief in the special place of variety in his plans. When visiting our son and his family in

Hawaii, I usually go snorkeling at least once. The numbers of fish species I see is astounding. It is often claimed that no two snowflakes are alike. (Of course, those making the claim must have done a rather enormous amount of research, and they will have to be satisfied with tentative conclusions at most.) God obviously is trying to tell us something important, even by the design of nature.

Spiritual thinking is colorblind in its absence of prejudice, but color-aware and color-appreciative in making us a family. I have often said that the ultimate effectiveness of spiritual leaders is found in their ability to lead different types of people. If we can only relate well or become emotionally close to people like us, we are missing out on one of the greatest possible blessings of life. May God grant you the perspective of family that he has taught the BBBs, for then your life will be enriched more than you can imagine! And thank you, my unique brothers of the club, for allowing me to be one of you in far more ways than simply being members of the same church. Praise God for his plan for his kingdom!

To Help You Focus

1.   What unspiritual ideas from your past have had to die in order for you to be in God's diverse family?

2. What have you learned from or how have you specifically been helped by those who are different from you?

3. In what ways do you need to apply Paul's principle of becoming all things to all men?

Spiritual Thinking Versus Doctrinal Thinking

> "Woe to you, teachers of the law and Pharisees, you hypocrites! You give a tenth of your spices—mint, dill and cumin. But you have neglected the more important matters of the law—justice, mercy and faithfulness. You should have practiced the latter, without neglecting the former."
>
> Matthew 23:23

I was raised in a religious group that majored in the minors and minored in the majors. The focus was on doctrine, doctrine and more doctrine. To our group, the road to heaven was paved with doctrinal accuracy, and we were absolutely paranoid about making the tiniest of mistakes in doctrinal matters. While declaring a commitment to the restoration of first century Christianity, we succeeded much more in restoring first century Pharisaism. One of our favorite warnings was from James 2:10, which states, "For whoever keeps the whole law and yet stumbles at just one point is guilty of breaking all of it." We lived in fear that we would miss just one little point of doctrine and thereby miss heaven. We understood neither James 2:10 nor the God who inspired it. Although we thought that our doctrinal emphasis was equivalent to spirituality, it was light-years from it.

However, there is something about the nature of man that easily becomes entangled in the web of a doctrinal focus. Read the following passages written to combat this very tendency in the first century: 1 Timothy 1:3-7; 2 Timothy 2:14-19; Titus 1:5-11, 3:3-11. When I find people who get into this doctrinal disposition, I know that something has gone awry in their hearts. One motivation for such a focus is a desire to be leaders, or leaders at levels they have not reached. In 1 Timothy 1:7, Paul wastes no words in putting them in their places: "They want to be teachers of the law, but they do not know what they are talking about or what they so confidently affirm." Another motivation for being doctrinally focused is to take the focus off sins in our personal lives. Often, those with this focus have relational problems or sin problems, and instead of being honest and facing the truth, they ride off on the horse of doctrinal concerns and disputation.

An amazing passage showing this latter tendency is found in Numbers 12:1-15. (Please take the time to read it before going further in this chapter.) Did you catch the real issue in verse 1 and then see the switch to doctrine beginning in verse two? (If not, read it again.) Several very important lessons are to be found here about the tendency to ride in on the horse of personal sin issues and out on the horse of doctrinal differences. The real issue with Aaron and Miriam was a personality conflict with Moses' wife, Zipporah.

> Miriam and Aaron began to talk against Moses because of his Cushite wife, for he had married a Cushite. (Numbers 12:1)

Looking further in the chapter, it seems likely that Miriam was really the main one with the sin, since she was the one smitten with leprosy, rather than her brother Aaron.

Keep in mind that we are talking about a brother and sister here—our tendency is to think that such things are quite understandable and expected when there is sibling rivalry. God did not have any such rationalization in mind, for Moses was his chosen leader, his top leader, who led the entire nation. Satan always works to undermine trust in God's top leaders. The doctrinal issue of who was to be the top prophet was not the real problem, although it was propounded to be.

> "Has the LORD spoken only through Moses?" they asked. "Hasn't he also spoken through us?" And the LORD heard this. (Numbers 12:2)

Obviously, the personality conflict was hidden behind a doctrinal issue, which is almost always the case. I saw it time and time again in my early years. Someone had a personality conflict with another person, and rather than admit it and work to resolve it, they fought and divided over a trumped-up doctrinal conflict. What a sad state of affairs! This human tendency in no way lessens the horror of this approach. It's no wonder that Jesus said that the unity of believers is the acid test of whether we are really his disciples (John 17:20-23).

The few divisions (thank you, Jesus, that they are *few*) that I have seen in God's modern day movement can all be traced back to a leader's ego run amok or to a smoke screen covering up personal sins. I know of absolutely no exceptions, in spite of vigorous denials of said leaders to the contrary. Division is itself sin, but it only comes as a symptom of deeper, and often hidden, sins.

God abhors division and the sins that lead up to it. In the case of Aaron and Miriam, notice God's immediate and decisive response. "The anger of the Lord burned against them, and he left them" (Numbers 12:9). Now that's a scary thought! Keep in mind that Aaron was the high priest of the nation and Miriam was perhaps the most influential woman leader. After God smote Miriam with leprosy, the brotherly sentimentality of both Aaron and Moses kicked in, and they pled for the removal of her disease. God, however, was not about to leave the issue without making a very strong point.

> The Lord replied to Moses, "If her father had spit in her face, would she not have been in disgrace for seven days? Confine her outside the camp for seven days; after that she can be brought back." (Numbers 12:14)

Imagine the embarrassment she must have felt during those seven days—and probably for the rest of her life. Yes, God has little patience with the sin of division and the underlying sins that lead up to it.

Therefore, when I encounter those who start down the path of doctrinal focus, my antennae vibrate with concern and the red flags go up. The traditional church out of which I came was characterized for decades by its doctrinal emphases and the sad tales of woe that resulted. A myriad of young people who might otherwise have grown up loving God simply walked away from the hypocrisy and dissension. I was one of those, and until I saw someone who understood both the grace and the purposes of God toward us humans, I gave up on church. Praise God that I found something better in the person of one unusual preacher when I was a young married man. Holding on to the ideals that he taught me kept me searching for a church like the one I read about in the Bible. Finally, when I discovered those committed to being disciples in 1981, I began to discover what true spirituality was all about: studying the Bible with a focus on personally being changed into the image of Jesus and helping others to change this way as well.

Of course, none of this is to say that doctrine is unimportant to God. Paul wrote,

> Watch your life and doctrine closely. Persevere in them, because if you do, you will save both yourself and your hearers. (1 Timothy 4:16)

"Doctrine" is simply the word in Greek (*didaskalia*) for "teaching." Hence, we must watch our teaching closely and make sure it contains the emphasis of God, which is to help us love him and love others with all of our hearts (Matthew 22:36-40). Several times in his evangelistic letters, Paul uses the term "*sound* doctrine" or "*sound* instruction" (1 Timothy 1:10, 6:3; 2 Timothy 1:13, 4:3; Titus 1:9, 13 and 2:1, emphasis added). This word (*hugiaino*) means "healthy." So, sound doctrine is that which makes the hearers spiritually healthy. Need it be added that those who become issues oriented are anything but spiritually and emotionally healthy? I recall the tense faces of the doctrinal disputants, appearing as if they had been weaned on dill pickles. The decibel level of some of their arguments suggested that "sound" doctrine was to them doctrine espoused with much emotionally laden noise.

May God help us to be truly healthy and to study the Bible deeply. We must always remember that our study is to help us understand the heart of our God and to imitate it. When we approach Bible study this way, the level of our gratitude and awe will soar, and our hearts will be filled with love for him and for the lost. We will want to teach his word, not in terms of doctrinal facts, as they are often conceived, but in terms of healthy principles that change lives. It is fine to question what all of the little details that we read in the Bible mean (or *meant* to the original recipients), but we can never allow our questions to lead us into majoring in the minors and vice versa.

Rest assured that spiritual thinking and doctrinal thinking are as different in their outcome as can be imagined. One leads to arrogance and the other to humility; one to heightened blood pressure, the other to inner peace; one to division, the other to other-worldly unity; one to hell, the other to heaven. Spiritual thinking is God-centered, and doctrinal thinking is man-centered. Spiritual thinking will always include a proper concern for doctrine. Doctrinal thinking will always become unspiritual, with neither a proper concern for God nor for our fellow man.

By the grace of God, let us remain on the narrow road that leads to life, and let us remember that it is a road characterized with spiritual thinking centered in the nature of God, rather than in worldly thinking centered on the ego of man.

To Help You Focus

1. When are you personally most tempted to argue a doctrinal issue? How can you use this information to help you in the future?

2. What is something new that you learned from reading the passage in Numbers? How about the New Testament passages regarding sound doctrine? How will you use these lessons in your life?

3. We cannot escape doctrinal discussions and even doctrinal disagreements, but how does spiritual thinking change the way we handle these?

16
Sentimentality—
Normal but Unspiritual

> "Enter through the narrow gate. For wide is
> the gate and broad is the road that leads to
> destruction, and many enter through it. But
> small is the gate and narrow the road that
> leads to life, and only a few find it....Not every-
> one who says to me, 'Lord, Lord,' will enter the
> kingdom of heaven, but only he who does the
> will of my Father who is in heaven."
>
> Matthew 7:13-14, 21

Are you saved or lost? Surely few questions have the
capacity to stir the emotions (and the pride) more. One of
our biggest challenges when dealing with the issue of
people's salvation is staying Biblical and not becoming
sentimental. Obviously, the issue is a highly important one,
because we first must ask ourselves about our own
salvation and be willing to come to grips with God's
answer. Once we have done this, we must ask the question
about the salvation of others, since we have been given a
commission from Jesus to seek and to save the lost. In view

of this commission, we must consider who is saved and who is lost.

When others suggested that we might be lost, especially if we viewed ourselves as saved, both our pride and our fears were engaged immediately. Having dealt with it ourselves, we have then watched many others we w re reaching out to go through the same feelings and reactions. No doubt the issue of who is saved and who is lost is close to the heart of any perceptive human being.

All of us at one time or another have struggled emotionally with thinking that certain people might be saved, although intellectually we thought that they probably were not. For example, it is common for people to ask about those in remote parts of the world who have never heard about Jesus. Are they lost simply because no one has shared the gospel with them? This question tugs at the heartstrings of us all. But sentimentality cannot answer the question; only the Bible can. For starters, if those who have never heard are saved in their ignorance, it would be cruel to enlighten them, because only a small minority of those who hear the message accept it. Why would Jesus give the Great Commission (Matthew 28:18-20) if people could be saved without it? Paul's statement in Acts 17:30 seems perfectly clear on the issue: "In the past God overlooked such ignorance, but now he commands all people everywhere to repent."

Actually, failure to hear the gospel and respond to it is not what causes people to be lost. Sin causes them to be lost. For example, if we saw someone drowning and failed to throw a life jacket to them, our failure would not be the cause of the drowning. They would drown because they were in the water and could not swim. They would fail to be saved because we did not throw the life jacket. Do you see the difference? Of course, since we have the means of rescue at our disposal, it is most urgent that we share it with as many who are drowning in sin as possible.

Some have appealed to Romans 2:14-15 to argue that the Gentiles are a law unto themselves and will be judged on the basis of their own consciences, rather than by God's law. Keep in mind that the overall thrust of Romans chapters 1-3 is to show that all have sinned and fall short of God's glory (Romans 3:23). Romans 1:18-32 definitively demonstrates the lost condition of the Gentiles, and then chapter 2 addresses the self-righteous Jews by using the example of Gentiles—who actually did better than most Jews at following what light they had. This doesn't mean that they were thereby saved, because no person has ever lived up to the standard of his own conscience. Thus, a law of conscience could ultimately excuse no one. However, previous to the cross, God did have dealings with Gentiles, such as when he sent Jonah to preach to the Ninevites. It would be logical to assume that Gentiles were afforded some means of having a relationship with him during this period of history, although the purpose of the Old Testament is not to enlighten us on that matter. After the cross, Paul's comments in Acts 17 remove any doubt about the spiritual condition of all now who are not Christians, whether Jew or Gentile.

Our sentimentality about the salvation of others comes into play most when we are contemplating the status of seemingly sincere religious people, especially if they are emotionally close to us. But again, the issue is not what we feel but what the Bible says. I remember having a chronic attack of such sentimentality some years back, as most do at times, and I began thinking about the logic of my tenuous view of others' salvation. In a nutshell, I applied my line of reasoning to my own baptismal experience. Would I be willing to meet God with the experience of infant baptism? It didn't take long to say, "Absolutely not!" Then I pictured myself having a so-called "believer's baptism," the type commonly taught by evangelicals (an outward sign of an inward grace—saved before baptism). Again, I certainly wouldn't want to meet God with that baptism, for it obviously differs in purpose from the one baptism described in the New Testament.

Let me interject a very important observation before going further. Baptism is not the gospel—Jesus' substitutionary death on the cross is the gospel (1 Corinthians 15:1-4). The gospel is God doing for us what we could not do for ourselves. Our acceptance of this message is based on our understanding that our only hope is in what he has done for us, not in what we do in response. God, who is totally righteous in character, can give us his righteousness ("right standing" with him) in Christ. Beyond that, he can develop righteous characters within us through his Holy Spirit. Both salvation and growth come from his grace, and our faith and commitment are responses to this grace. He never says, "Measure up and I'll accept you." He always says, "I'll accept you in Christ (by virtue of the cross), and now let's walk the path of life together."

Bottom line, it is the grace of God that saves us (Romans 3:24), makes us strong (2 Timothy 2:1) and motivates us to work hard (1 Corinthians 15:10). Therefore, when our heads *understand* grace and our hearts *feel* grace, then our lives will *demonstrate* grace in action. Many of us need a much better understanding of the grace of God—and the difference between obedience out of love and appreciation and obedience out of duty. No matter how well we may obey, we are still unworthy sinners who need to stand amazed that God would even want us in his family. Praise him for his unbelievable, unfathomable grace!

Having said all this, it is still important that we understand the proper place of baptism in our faith acceptance of Christ, for Paul is quite clear on the fact that there is only one baptism acceptable to God (Ephesians 4:5). Only the death of Jesus merits our forgiveness, but baptism is clearly an essential part of our accepting this forgiveness. While we cannot get "hung up" on doctrine, neither can we allow sentimentality or lack of deep convictions to lead us away from any truth in Scripture.

The final step in the process of examining my own sentimental tendencies was to think about my own original baptism in the mainline Church of Christ. At age thirteen, I was baptized out of fear of going to hell. Without question, I was taught that baptism was for the forgiveness of sins, but that alone does not make a baptism valid. The baptism of the New Testament must be preceded by repentance (Acts 2:38), which is tantamount to making the decision to be a disciple of Jesus (Matthew 28:19). This decision must have two components: to cease doing wrong and to begin doing right—both as defined by the Scriptures.

I had in mind to repent of the bad, but I had little idea of what being a disciple really entailed. As a result, I did not even follow through with the cessation of the bad. In terms of Matthew 12:43-45, I tried sweeping out the evil, but did not fill my house with the good. I ended up with "seven demons" coming into my life, as I did worse things than ever for many years. So, I had to ask myself if I would be willing to meet God after a baptism that meant nothing more than this. The answer to that one is all too clear, since I was baptized again, even after preaching for many years in that same group.

Therefore, if I would not be willing to meet God with any of those man-defined baptisms, why would I even contemplate allowing others to do it? This reasoning process dispelled my sentimentality.

Taking such a firm stand on the salvation issue arouses the displeasure of just about all other religious groups, resulting in our being called narrow-minded and judgmental by leaders in those groups. But who is really judgmental? They make the judgment that God is going to be broader in his judgment than his word indicates. Being "broader" than the Bible puts you on the wrong road. I do not want to be broader or narrower than Jesus in my thinking. It is true that we are not the judges on the Final Day, but God will be the Judge, and he has already given us the basis of his judgment (John 12:48). I am willing to let him be Judge, and if he lets people into heaven whose salvation I questioned, no one will be more delighted than I. Certainly, none of us has any pleasure in the thought of others being condemned.

I have two overriding concerns about two potential extremes regarding our thinking about who is lost and who is saved. One is that we get caught up in truly being judgmental and reasoning like the Pharisee, who thought that he had the truth locked up in a wee, small box—and only he had the key to all the locks! We are not the judges of the universe; only God is. I remember one old preacher comparing our job to that of a policeman, who has the law and must point it out in no uncertain terms to those who violate it. Ultimately, the judge in the courtroom will make the final dispositions in their cases, and he can decide to exert clemency if he chooses. However, the policeman's job is to point out what the law actually says, and he has absolutely no right to tell a violator that the judge will or will not exert clemency—he can only point people to what the law demands.

Concern number two is that we will lose our conviction that being religious doesn't necessarily equate with salvation. Both extremes are un-Biblical and dangerous, and both will ultimately undermine the carrying out of the Great Commission. If we lose our distinctiveness in teaching Biblical salvation, including an understanding both of the grace behind it and the means of accepting it, we lose our moorings as a movement. We cannot allow sentimentality to cause us to think or intimate to others that God will do things differently than what the Bible seems to clearly teach. We must stick to sharing it, leaving the final judgment to God on that Day of days. Until then, we are to teach his word and assure others that following the Bible exactly cannot be questionable. Following it inexactly is certainly questionable, so why think of doing it?

Sentimentality and spiritual thinking do not go together. The same is true of sentimentality and the narrow road to heaven. Do not allow others to meet God with a conversion process that you would not trust for yourself. Surely God cannot fault us with this approach to persuading others, for it is the obviously safe way.

To Help You Focus

1. Why is it important to have convictions about who is lost and who is saved? What happens to a church that loses these convictions?

2. Why is it equally important to not be the Pharisee who
    has everything about God and his judgments locked in
    his small box?

3. In what situations are you most vulnerable to sentimen-
    tality? How can other disciples help you with that
    challenge?

Heaven Can Wait!

> For to me, to live is Christ and to die is gain. If I am to go on living in the body, this will mean fruitful labor for me. Yet what shall I choose? I do not know! I am torn between the two: I desire to depart and be with Christ, which is better by far; but it is more necessary for you that I remain in the body.
>
> Philippians 1:21-24

One of my favorite comedy movies has the same title as this chapter. The star's character was killed in the beginning of the movie, and he was very disturbed to find himself at the entrance of heaven rather than playing professional football back on earth. In essence, he says that heaven can wait awhile, for he has many important things to do on earth. (This beginning shows us a lot about our American values, doesn't it?) So, he enters the body of a dying man and is able to come back into the world that he loves. I wonder how many of us have about the same view of heaven—that it is sort of a consolation prize, not as good as earth, but certainly better than hell. We have much to learn about spiritual thinking.

Paul's statement in Philippians 1 gives us an entirely different view. He longed for heaven, but was willing to wait in order to fulfill his purpose on earth: the task of reaching more and more people for Jesus. You see, Paul knew what lay on the other side of death—he had seen it. (2 Corinthians 12:2-7 describes his vision of eternity.) No wonder death held no fear for him, and heaven was so real! We need to borrow his faith in order to gain his perspective of life and death, heaven and hell. However, when we are thinking, "Heaven can wait," we are more like the star of the movie than the star of the New Testament letters, the apostle Paul.

About a year ago, a sister on the ministry staff of the Boston church asked me to read a diary written by a relative of hers from the last century. After some months, I decided to take the time to read it. The writer, a frontier woman of the 1800s, recorded her life's history in sketchy but touching terms. Sarah Ann Cromer was born May 3, 1815, married January 27, 1832, "got religion" August 18, 1833, and died about 1880.

When I finished reading the little diary, my emotions welled up, and I just sat down and cried. As I tried to figure out why, I thought about what stood out in her story. It boiled down to three emphases that came up repeatedly. First, she read her Bible over and over again. One entry would read, "Finished the Testament today," and another would state, "Began the Bible over again today." Second, her life was filled with tragedy, as were most lives in that period. Her health failed, her children died and everyone went through a horrible and most uncivil conflict between brothers, the Civil War. Third, from her earliest years, she was amazingly focused on heaven. Over and over she reminded her children that "Momma was going to heaven" and that they should live in such a way as to meet her over there. There is much about this woman I cannot know, but I know in her struggle she saw some things far more clearly than most people do today. We were made for the very purpose of going to heaven (2 Corinthians 5:5). She got that one right.

Were it not for that little diary, complete with its misspellings and poor grammar, almost no one today would know that this simple woman ever existed. It will be much the same for us after a century has passed. Who of us knows their great-great grandparents' names or life stories? Life goes by so quickly. As the psalmist said,

> The length of our days is seventy years—
>   or eighty, if we have the strength;
> yet their span is but trouble and sorrow,
>   for they quickly pass, and we fly away.
> (Psalm 90:10)

The Bible is filled with verses describing the brevity of life, and they are there for the purpose of reminding us not to invest our lives in endeavors that death will take away. (See Job 7:6-7; 8:9; 9:25-26; 14:1-2; Psalm 39:4-6; 39:11; 78:39; 89:47-48; 102:11; 103:14-16—to limit ourselves to only two Biblical books.) We are all destined to become but dim memories in the minds of those whom we leave behind. Praise God that heaven cannot wait for us! "Precious in the sight of the Lord is the death of his saints" (Psalm 116:15).

As I contemplated the impact of the little diary, perhaps my favorite brief passage of Scripture in the Bible, 2 Corinthians 4:16-18, came to mind. I have based many of my sermons on it and shared it with those facing death a number of times. It reads:

> Therefore we do not lose heart. Though outwardly we are wasting away, yet inwardly we are being renewed day by day. For our light and momentary troubles are achieving for us an eternal glory that far outweighs them all. So we fix our eyes not on what is seen, but on what is unseen. For what is seen is temporary, but what is unseen is eternal.

It would seem the simple frontier woman understood the passage. She was inwardly renewed daily by reading and meditating on the Bible. She faced her troubles with heaven's perspective that they were brief and light. Finally, she kept her mind and heart focused on the unseen world beyond this life. How desperately we need to do the same.

In bygone centuries, people's lives were filled with hardship in measures that most of us can only imagine. They had little to look forward to in life and as a result, focused on what lay beyond the grave. We, on the other hand, have so much materially that life seems much better than it actually is. It is easy to become far too attached to this life and to feel that heaven can wait as long as possible. To think spiritually is to see this life for the temporary thing that it is and to see heaven as that which is really worth living for.

Recently I sat on a beautiful beach and gazed at the surrounding beauty for a long time, thinking about God, my life and eternity. As the beauties of creation shouted out the glory of God, a thought struck my heart: *As beautiful as all of this is, God made it as a throwaway.* It has a temporary purpose and is destined to be burned up and to pass away (2 Peter 3:10). If this grandeur-filled universe is only to be discarded when its purpose is over, just what must heaven be like?

I shared this thought recently with an audience of physically challenged disciples. They were much more receptive to the message than we able-bodied folk tend to be. Life for them is tough, and most of them must fight for joy through their pain. But they remind me that I am a TAB (Temporarily Able-Bodied person), and I know they are right. Before our lives are over, most of us are going to face some huge challenges, and the only way I know to handle them with grace is to keep my eyes focused on heaven.

Once, when our son, Bryan, was a little boy scooting about the house, my father made a comment that I have never forgotten. As he looked at me and at Bryan, he said, "Son, one day before long, the cycle of life will have its way. You will be in my place as the grandfather, Bryan will be the dad, another little kid will be running around the house, and I will be gone." Well, Dad was right. He is gone, Bryan is thirty-two (amazingly!), and Bryce Gordon is the toddler running around. A few months back, I reminded Bryan of Pop's comment, and then I repeated it from my vantage point: "Soon I will be gone, you will be the grandfather, Bryce will be the father, and yet another generation of children will be toddling around beneath your feet."

Do you get the point? Do you think I am being morbid or morose? We are all speeding toward the Judgement Day and eternity beyond it, and most of us are far too focused on other things. What really matters except heaven and everything that contributes meaningfully to it?

We need to lift up our eyes and fix them on the unseen, for it is that destination for which we have been designed. This life is a very temporary proving ground for our faith, a physical habitat to hone our appreciation and anticipation for the spiritual reality to which all of life points. If you miss the focus, you may well miss the place. Heaven waits for us. Let's wait for it with a longing to meet our Creator and Savior, to enter the realm for which we are created, to rejoice in the love of God, while the ages roll on, world without end. Heaven *can't* wait!

To Help You Focus

1. What do you think heaven will be like? Jot down some ideas. How does your view line up with the Scriptures?

2. How does a focus on heaven impact your life and especially your view of trials?

3. What in this world seems better than heaven to you? What does Scripture teach about whatever you might have said?

18
Even Though..., God!

> By faith Abraham, when called to go to a place he would later receive as his inheritance, obeyed and went, *even though* he did not know where he was going....By faith Abraham, *even though* he was past age—and Sarah herself was barren—was enabled to become a father because he considered him faithful who had made the promise....By faith Abraham, when God tested him, offered Isaac as a sacrifice. He who had received the promises was about to sacrifice his one and only son, *even though* God had said to him, "It is through Isaac that your offspring will be reckoned." Abraham reasoned that God could raise the dead, and figuratively speaking, he did receive Isaac back from death.
>
> Hebrews 11:8, 11, 17-20
> (emphasis added)

Life is chock-full of challenges, and it's no less so for those who have named Jesus as Lord. In fact, additional challenges come our way because we wear that name. Sometimes the challenges are light in nature and are even mercifully spaced out, but sometimes they come at us fast and furious. What are we to do when life seems overwhelming? How can we keep on going when desired changes seem impossible? Where are we to turn when the answers to our dilemmas seem unavailable?

To find some answers to these questions, a look at the life of Abraham, as described in Hebrews 11, is a good starting place. Three times his challenges appeared monumental, and three times he found the solution. In each case, the solution was the same—right thinking about God. His first call to follow God came when he was living in Ur of the Chaldees (Acts 7:2-4). Archaeological excavations have shown that this city was one of the most advanced of its time, even boasting running water in many of the dwellings. (Keep in mind that many in America did not have such conveniences as late as the last century!) When Abraham left what may well have been the lap of luxury, he didn't even know where he was going—no travel itinerary was provided nor were accommodations reserved.

After spending time in Haran, he was called again to leave for Canaan. Once in this new land, the supposed land of milk and honey, he lived as a nomad in tents. This way of life was a far cry from the luxuries of Ur. The fact that he did eventually amass some wealth did not change the sacrificial lifestyle that he had been called to. He essentially camped out for the rest of his life as a stranger in a foreign land, far from the rest of his family (except for Lot). Compared to what he once enjoyed, the depth of his sacrifices likely went far beyond what we normally assume. How did he adjust to all of this? Even though life was challenging, by faith he believed deeply that God was holding his hand through those challenges and would provide all of the needed solutions as time marched on.

The next hurdle for Abraham's faith described in Hebrews 11 was the promise that he would be the father of one through whom the world would ultimately be blessed. He was old and his wife was definitely past the age of childbearing. In the words of Romans 4:18, "Against all hope, Abraham in hope believed." Further, "he faced the fact that his body was as good as dead—since he was about a hundred years old—and that Sarah's womb was also dead" (Romans 4:19). He was no blind idealist, for he did *face* the facts, but because he was a spiritual idealist, he then "faithed" the facts! What was and what could be were two quite different things in his heart.

In an earlier book *The Victory of Surrender* I described the next episode of Abraham's faith challenges.

> In my mind, the high-water mark of Abraham's faith came some years later when God commanded him to sacrifice this beloved son. In Genesis 22:3, it says, "early the next morning" Abraham set out on his journey to kill Isaac. Amazing! If I had been he, I would have postponed the whole process as long as possible. But not Abraham. He searched for reasons to trust God. In our logical humanism, we often look for reasons not to trust. Note in Hebrews 11:19 that "Abraham reasoned that God could raise the dead, and figuratively speaking, he did receive

Isaac back from death." The Bible does not call his response "faith" specifically, because Biblical faith is based on the word of God (Romans 10:17), and in this instance, God did not tell him what the ultimate plan was.

However, Abraham clung to two fundamental truths from God. One, he knew Isaac was the son of promise through whom his lineage would multiply. Two, he knew God had commanded his death. From a human perspective, the situation made no sense at all. A sermon based on this event could be titled "When God Contradicts God." But Abraham reasoned with a childlike trust that he would kill his son, and then God would simply raise him from the dead. In spite of the monumental challenge of killing one's own son, the man took it in stride because nothing in his life was held back from God. His surrender was absolute. The Lord's verdict in the matter? "Now I know that you fear God, because you have not withheld from me your son, your only son" (Genesis 22:12). James added this postscript to the record about Abraham: "...and he was called God's friend" (James 2:23).

Why did the Biblical writers use the example of Abraham so often and in so much detail? Surely not just to provide us with some interesting reading. We, in our humanity, have extreme difficulty walking by faith instead of sight, and those who have gone before us are proof that it can be done. We can rise above the level of mediocrity and failure. We do not have to be stuck in our ruts of human frailties. Even though life's challenges are great, God is able to provide the solutions and the victories. But we will not be victorious if we sacrifice our faith on the altar of reason, logic or cynicism. God is bigger than what appears to be, or even what actually *is*. He created the laws of the universe, but he is not bound by them. He can do what he wants, when he wants, any way that he wants and to whom he wants. It is time to break out of our "grasshopper" thinking (Numbers 13:33) and quit imagining that we are facing giants. Man's extremities are God's opportunities.

When people are studying to become disciples, they make some radical changes that often shock those who know them well. How do they make the changes? By faith in a God who smashes our limitations. But after we have been Christians for a few years, we often seem stuck in our character weaknesses and our life situations. Why is this? Our faith has eroded, plain and simple. We may have delightedly approached the marriage altar on our wedding days only to find ourselves in the all-too-common situation a few years later of feeling that our lot in life is simply to endure relational challenges that seem impervious to change. Where did our nuptial idealism go? In a word, we lost it in the land of doubt and unbelief. We have given up and given in, and it shows on our faces and in the faces of our children who cannot escape the inevitable conse-quences of our lack of faith. What a heartbreak!

Folks, it is time to get back the idealism that belongs to faith in God. We can change, and then change some more! Our marriages can change; our children can change; our hearts can change. We just can't give up. The same God who left Abraham staggering by what he was able to do is still here today. He longs to bless you. He lives to help you change and grow and succeed in your faith. Don't give up on him and don't give up on yourself—or on anyone else. It may take ten years to convert a loved one, and for sure it will take a persevering faith.

Never give up and never give in, for he is emphatically on your side. Think spiritually. Look with the eyes of faith. To all of your challenges, you must say again and again, "Even though..., God!" Then you will find yourself walking in the steps once more of the one called the father of the faithful, Abraham. Remember that the eternal, limitless God is the father of your spirit and your future. Trust him, and you will replace the limitations of unbelief with a faith that can remove all of your mountains.

To Help You Focus

1. Were there any new insights into Abraham's life and faith that struck you? What new faith have you gained from looking at Abraham?

2. What situation in your life is the most difficult for you to look at with eyes of faith?

3. How can you be sure that God does not have the same view of those facts as you may have?

4. Write out a Hebrews 11-type verse and include your name and the phrase "even though."

Epilogue
When You Get Where You're Going, Where Will You Be?

The way you think determines the daily course of your life. More importantly, it determines your course over the long haul. Character is built one day at a time, which means that weak character can be strengthened as we make spiritual choices—and strong character can be weakened if we make unspiritual ones. "Little things mean a lot," said an old song, and certainly this is true when it comes to the effects of our thinking and doing. What seems but a small, momentary decision can lead to consequences far beyond the moment, because each decision becomes a part of shaping our characters. A rifle aimed at a target two hundred yards away may be off the mark by only a very small amount at the ten-foot mark, but when the bullet covers the distance to the target, it may miss the bull's-eye by a wide margin. The importance of making righteous decisions consistently, without becoming the least bit careless, cannot be overstated. Your life will end up at the target toward which it is aimed now. So, when *you* get where *you're* going, where will you be?

For many years, I have observed the truth of this principle in the lives of older people. Some are like the proverbial grandmother who brings cookies and milk with the sweetest of smiles. They are very warm and light-hearted, a real joy to be around. But honestly, just how many older people do you encounter who are like this? Not many, if your experience is anything like mine.

A few years ago, I knocked doors for our HOPE Outreach Day and talked to a number of older people in a certain area of the city in which we were working. Most were either very sad or very cynical—or both. I still remember one older, grandmotherly woman who answered the door and brought sunshine out with her. Meeting her was, in comparison to most we met, like finding a rose in a smelly trash can. She definitely stood out.

You see, older people have reached the target at which they have been aimed for years and years, as far as characters and attitudes go. The thinking that characterized them for years reaches its conclusion, be it kind or bitter. When you get where you're going, where will you be?

Keeping our minds focused on the positive and spiritual in life is not easy. But with God's help, we can learn to do it! Paul provides us with an amazing example of seeing the hand of God in everything, every day. Even while chained to prison guards, he was almost beside himself with joy-filled thinking. A cursory reading of Philippians demonstrates this clearly. One of my favorite passages in this little, happy book is found in chapter 4.

> Rejoice in the Lord always. I will say it again: Rejoice! Let your gentleness be evident to all. The Lord is near. Do not be anxious about anything, but in everything, by prayer and petition, with thanksgiving, present your requests to God. And the peace of God, which transcends all understanding, will guard your hearts and your minds in Christ Jesus.
>
> Finally, brothers, whatever is true, whatever is noble, whatever is right, whatever is pure, whatever is lovely, whatever is admirable—if anything is excellent or praiseworthy—think about such things. Whatever you have learned or received or heard from me, or seen in me—put it into practice. And the God of peace will be with you. (Philippians 4:4-9)

Here, God tells us to rejoice, which means (1) that the decision is ours, and (2) we *can* do it. Paul is essentially saying, "Just loosen up, and trust that the Lord is near and in control your life's circumstances." Refuse to allow the practical atheism of anxiety to control your thinking. Instead, pour out your hearts in prayer to him, bathing your heart in gratitude. Remember that the key to the future is the past; for if God has protected and provided in the past, surely he will not neglect to do so in the future. As an older man now, I appreciate more than ever the observation of David in Psalm 37:25.

> I was young and now I am old,
> > yet I have never seen the righteous forsaken
> or their children begging bread.

Our Philippians passage goes on to promise us that God's peace becomes better felt than told when we have this trust in our hearts. Just keep your mind engaged with the positives of loving and serving God and others, and imitate those who have learned these lessons. Then the God of peace will be with you in life and in death, for time and for eternity, during the moments of mountaintop exhilaration and also during the valley-low moments of heartache.

> "The Lord himself goes before you and will be with you; he will never leave you nor forsake you. Do not be afraid; do not be discouraged." (Deuteronomy 31:8)

When you get where you're going, where will you be? It all depends on the path your thinking is taking you on, day by day, month by month, year by year. Before you know it, we will all be standing before the God of the universe, giving an account of how we have lived our brief lives on his earth. How we feel then will be determined by how we feel now—and all feeling is a result of your thinking and doing, every day in every way.

You and I are aimed at a target right now, and we will all reach it sooner than we can imagine. "Therefore, prepare your minds for action; be self-controlled; set your hope fully on the grace to be given you when Jesus Christ is revealed" (1 Peter 1:13). The power of spiritual thinking: a life lived for God in time and a soul with its Maker in eternity. Don't miss it!

Who Are We?

Discipleship Publications International (DPI) began publishing in 1993. We are a nonprofit Christian publisher affiliated with the International Churches of Christ, committed to publishing and distributing materials that honor God, lift up Jesus Christ and show how his message practically applies to all areas of life. We have a deep conviction that no one changes life like Jesus and that the implementation of his teaching will revolutionize any life, any marriage, any family and any singles household.

Since our beginning, we have published more than 100 titles; plus, we have produced a number of important, spiritual audio products. More than one million volumes have been printed, and our works have been translated into more than a dozen languages—international is not just a part of our name! Our books are shipped regularly to every inhabited continent.

To see a more detailed description of our works, find us on the World Wide Web at www.dpibooks.org. You can order books by calling 1-888-DPI-BOOK twenty-four hours a day. From outside the US, call 781-937-3883, ext. 231 during Boston-area business hours.

We appreciate the hundreds of comments we have received from readers. We would love to hear from you. Here are other ways to get in touch:

Mail: DPI, One Merrill St., Woburn, MA 01801
E-Mail: dpibooks@icoc.org

Find Us on the World Wide Web

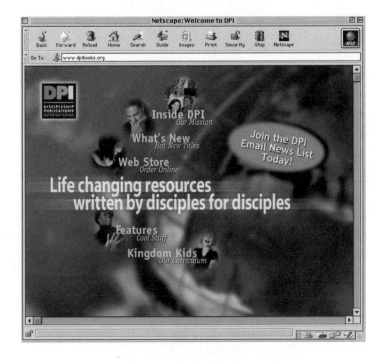

www.dpibooks.org
1-888-DPI-BOOK
outside US: 781-937-3883 x231